ETH...

A. C. EWING

ETHICS

THE FREE PRESS
A Division of Macmillan Publishing Co., Inc.
New York

Copyright © 1953 by A. C. Ewing

All rights reserved. No part of this book may be reproduced or transmitted in any form or by any means, electronic or mechanical, including photocopying, recording or by any information storage and retrieval system, without permission in writing from the Publisher.

The Free Press
A Division of Macmillan Publishing Co., Inc.
866 Third Avenue, New York, N.Y. 10022

FIRST FREE PRESS PAPERBACK EDITION 1965

Printed in the United States of America

printing number

10

Contents

	Preface	7
1.	Introductory	9
2.	Selfishness and Unselfishness	21
3.	The Pursuit of the General Happiness	36
4.	Duty for Duty's Sake	49
5.	The Pursuit of the Good	61
6.	Attempts to Define "Good" and "Ought"	78
7.	The Nature of Ethical "Judgement"	102
8.	Deserts and Responsibility	126
	Bibliography	158
	Index	159

Preface

There is a strong tendency to-day to identify knowledge with natural science. But, as two wars have made us painfully aware, natural science can only tell us the means, not how these means ought to be used, so that we may well be in the end only the worse off for our science. The study of science must therefore be supplemented by a study of the right way of using the knowledge it provides. In so far as we are moral beings we must all pay some attention to this study; the attempts of the ablest thinkers to pursue it in the most comprehensive way and in a spirit as scientific, if by methods very different from those of the natural sciences, are here recorded and criticized.

A. C. Ewing,
Trinity Hall,
Cambridge.

Chapter 1

Introductory

YOU, READER, whoever you are, are not a complete beginner in this subject. You already have some idea what "good" and "bad," "right" and "wrong" mean, and you know some acts to be right, others wrong, some things to be good and some bad. Now these are precisely the topics with which Ethics as a subject of systematic study deals. Further, if you did not already have this knowledge, you could not make a start on the subject at all. Ethics is concerned with two main kinds of question, first, with deciding the general principles on which ethical terms, i.e. good, bad, duty, etc., are to be applied to anything, and secondly with deciding precisely what these terms mean. Now there seems to be no possibility of validly deducing ethical propositions by some sort of logical argument from the nature of reality without first assuming some ethical propositions to be true; or at least if there is, the way to do so has not yet been discovered by anybody. This may be a disappointing conclusion, but it is borne out by the whole trend of philosophical thought on the subject. Consequently the only way in which we can develop a systematic theory of Ethics is by starting with the ethical judgements which we find ourselves in our practical thinking constrained to make. To these is often given the name, *common-sense ethics,* and I shall distinguish from this *systematic ethics* as a subject of study by writing the latter with a capital E.

That Ethics should start with common-sense ethics does not of course mean that it should stop there. For one thing, the ordinary practical ethical judgements to which I am referring are each concerned with a particular situation, but Ethics like science seeks to generalize. We have indeed all made some advance in that direction at a very early age. There are quite a number of ethical generalizations, such as that it is wrong to steal, which we have learnt at our mother's knee, but the student of Ethics is not content with these, he wishes to make further generalizations, and especially he wishes to give the reasons why the generalizations are true and decide which are the most ultimate. Further, he may as the result of his studies come to the conclusion that some of our ordinary generalizations and some of our particular ethical judgements ought to be amended. Certainly, though he may take common-sense ethics as his starting-point, he must not regard the latter as infallible. He could not indeed do this without absurdity, since the common-sense ethics of one civilization is liable to contradict that of another, and the same often applies even to two men within the same civilization. But I do not see how we can correct a common-sense ethical judgement without reference to some other ethical judgement, since unless we first admit the validity of some ethical judgements we have no means of proving any ethical judgement.

How are we to proceed then? It seems to me that the analogy of physical science is here very helpful, far removed as its specific methods are from the methods of Ethics. In science men originally started with ordinary perceptions of physical objects and the judgements expressing them. Then on this basis they developed a theory of the physical world which not only went far beyond their perceptions but refuted and corrected these in many respects, as when it told us that the earth was round and the sun very much larger than the earth, though they by no means look so. Yet in the last resort all physical science is absolutely dependent on our perceptions. We could never have started to form a scientific conception of physical things if we could not perceive them, and even the most recondite investigations by which Einstein's theory is confirmed depend on the scientist trusting his ordinary sense-perception when he observes physical objects. Even if cameras and automatic recording machines are used to act as substitutes for human sense-organs, somebody must observe the photographs and other records and trust his senses that he has observed them aright. How then can physical science contradict human perceptions when it can only proceed by trusting our perceptions? The answer is that the object of science is to build up that system which will best account for our perceptions and knit the judgements based on them together into a consistent whole in which the different parts do not contradict but confirm each other. In order to attain the system which of those at our disposal will explain our experience best and give us a rationally connected picture of the world, the sciences and indeed common-sense are constrained to reject certain of our perceptions as illusory in order to be able consistently to give reality to others. Thus even before studying science we reject for such reasons the apparent perceptions that we call dreams.

Now Ethics pursues the same end as regards the judgements of common-sense ethics. These can all be regarded as expressing perceptions of something real but as liable to be distorted by various circumstances. And just as the scientist may, though starting from sense-perceptions and confirming his conclusions by sense-perceptions, reject many of our perceptions as giving an inaccurate picture of things, so the writer on Ethics may, while starting from our ordinary ethical judgements, require the amendment of some of these judgements in order to fit in with others more important and to make up an intelligible coherent system in his own field. He will not, I think, have to reject as illusory nearly so large a proportion of ethical judgements as the scientist does of physical perceptions. The test in either case is not whether our final view just reproduces what we seem to perceive at the common-sense level, but whether it with the aid of these perceptions makes up a really coherent system which, while explaining why we made any errors we did make in our ordinary judgements, helps us to see better what is true in these judgements. This is all very abstract, but it is hardly possible to illustrate it by examples till we have dealt with at least one of the particular ethical systems put forward in the past by thinkers. And in applying the test we shall, I think, just be carrying further the same process of ethical thinking in which we all engage when we try to make up our minds rationally as to what is right. It is a very attractive feature of this subject that, since we can all think ethically, we have in our own minds the means of testing the theories with which we are presented. No expensive laboratory or difficult mathematical technique is needed in order intelligently to discuss Ethics.

Again, we could not intelligently make any ethical judgements of any sort if we had not some understanding of the meaning of terms like good, duty, etc., yet it is a vital part of the business of Ethics to define their meaning as far as this is possible. So Ethics must in this respect also be regarded as completing a task which we have already begun before studying it at all. We have some idea of what "good," etc., mean before opening a single book on Ethics, yet Ethics helps us to understand their meaning better than we did before we studied it.

The two main ethical concepts are expressed respectively by the words "good" and "ought" (or "duty"). But these terms, especially the former, are very far from unambiguous, being in fact used in a variety of different senses, and it is necessary to distinguish one or two of these before starting. Particularly important is the distinction between good as a means and good as an end. If you are suffering from an illness it may be good for you to have an operation, but this certainly does not mean that it is in any way desirable as an end in itself, it only signifies that it is good in the sense of being a means to produce something else which is good. In this case the end is health. It may however be doubted whether even health is good in itself. We should not care whether our teeth were decayed or our appendix inflamed or not if we could be sure that the decay and inflammation would neither hurt us nor make us less efficient in engaging in any activity. This suggests that health is good only as a means to happiness and to any other ends we may seek to pursue in our activities. But there are some things, e.g. happiness and virtue, which seem to be good in their own right and not merely because they produce something else which is good. Practically everybody would value at least happiness even if it never produced any advantages beyond itself, provided only it did not do harm, and very many at least would take the same view about virtue. These things are called good-in-themselves, good as ends, or intrinsically good. Obviously this kind of goodness is more fundamental than the other. Something which is merely good as a means can be rationally valued only because it is liable to produce something else which is intrinsically good (or diminish something intrinsically evil as e.g. medicines diminish pain). On the other hand something that is good as a means may also be good as an end, and it is all the better if this is so. Thus kindness may be commended both because it is good in itself and because it produces happiness. The distinction between ends and means must therefore not be taken too rigidly. The very qualities which make virtue good as an end make it good as a means also. Further, we may easily come to love and prize for its own sake something that we originally valued only for its effects and still admit would have no value if it were not for these effects. The miser takes this attitude to his wealth, and we almost all take it in some degree to some particularly useful material objects. On this ground the distinction between end and means has been sharply attacked, e.g. by the American philosopher, John Dewey. But the question is not what we actually prize, it is what are the ultimate grounds why it is reasonable to prize it, and these can only be found in what is an end in itself, not what is merely a means.

People are liable to ask about everything—What is the use of it?—meaning—To what future end is it a good means? But unless some things were good-in-themselves and not only as means, nothing would be of any use at all. To value everything only as a means would be to do everything for the sake of a future benefit which never came. The two mistakes of taking for granted that, because work is useful, it necessarily cannot also be appreciated as an activity of value in itself, and of assuming that oneself and others ought always to be doing something "useful" have, I am sure, resulted in a great unnecessary loss of happiness. In saying this I am not denying that all too many kinds work can hardly be enjoyed for their own sake, and that it is all the better if the things we enjoy doing for their own sake are also beneficial educationally in a wide sense of "education" (except in so far as it is too much of a strain to be always being "educated"). Many things are well worth doing in themselves apart from their utility for anything else, though they may also be useful.

Nor must we look at a purposive process under the category of means and end in a way which represents the earlier part as necessarily simply a means to the later as an end-in-itself. From this point of view logically carried out it would follow that a book was written simply for the sake of being able to say Finis. Throughout there will be parts that are of value only as means, parts which are of value only as ends-in-themselves, and parts which are of value in both ways. The earlier part may be both a means and an end, and the later is not necessarily in the sense under discussion an end. The return from the theatre in a crowded bus is just as liable to be a valueless but necessary part of a process, other parts of which have value, as the going there, which is admittedly only a means.

It is generally agreed among those who have thought on the subject that, with the possible exception of beautiful objects, valuable on account of their beauty, a merely physical thing cannot be good in itself but only good as a means. Apart at least from the very doubtful exception just mentioned, what is good in itself must be an experience, state of mind or life, it cannot be anything without consciousness at all.

Now to determine whether something is good as a means we require the kind of knowledge which is pursued in natural science, namely, a knowledge of the laws of nature and so of the effects things are likely to produce. But this knowledge, we must insist, is useless for deciding whether something is good-in-itself. We clearly cannot learn this merely by learning that it produces something else good. It is the knowledge of what is good or bad in itself, and not the knowledge of the goodness of means which falls within Ethics. The natural sciences teach us what is good as a means, but ethically they are neutral in the sense that the same scientific knowledge which is used, e.g. to cure a patient, may be used by a bad man to kill the patient. Recent history has instructed us sufficiently in the lesson that scientific knowledge is a curse to the world and not a blessing if its results are utilized without regard to the principles of ethics. There are many other different senses of "good," but these are the only two we need now distinguish.

The term "ought" differs from "good" in referring primarily to actions. It is sometimes used to signify merely the best means to take to a given end irrespective of whether the end is good or bad, as in e.g. "the murderer ought not to have left his fingerprints on the weapon," but the use in which it is applied to the really best action for an agent to choose in a given moral situation is ethically of much greater importance, and it is in this sense that I shall be using the word in the following chapters, unless I say anything to the contrary. It is one of the chief questions of Ethics what are the ultimate criteria for deciding which actions we ought to do in this sense. The action that we ought to do is also called our "duty," but there is another sense of both "ought" and "duty" of which I shall speak later[1] according to which we are said to do our duty or what we ought in cases where we do what we think is our duty but are honestly mistaken as to our objective duty. Another equivalent of "the action we ought to do" is "the right action," but "right" when used without the definite article has a slightly different meaning. For there might in a given situation be alternative actions which were all right, but it could not be the case that there were two incompatible actions *both* of which we ought to do or which it was our duty to do. Thus it is ordinarily right to pay one's debts by cheque, but not a duty because it is also right to pay them by cash. Our duty is to pay them somehow (either by cheque or by cash or by some other method, e.g. deduction from a bill of ours on the creditor).

[1] *v.* below p. 126 ff.

In order to decide what action we ought to take or it is right to take in a given situation, one at least of the questions we ought to ask is what the consequences of any proposed action will be. It is a disputed question among writers on Ethics whether the rightness of an action depends solely on its consequences or not, but certainly it depends at least partly on them. It is always an objection to performing a certain act that it will produce bad effects, whether it is always a completely conclusive objection or sometimes may be outweighed by other considerations. So in order to decide whether we ought to do something or not we either always or at least usually need to have a knowledge of what the consequences of the action are likely to be. This is knowledge of the type obtained by natural science, as is the knowledge which enables us to decide whether something is a good means to a given end. To obtain it what we need to know is what are the relevant causal laws. It is in itself not specifically ethical knowledge at all. But this knowledge is not sufficient: we need also to know whether the consequences anticipated are to be regarded as good or bad in themselves. Thus the decision as to what we ought to do depends partly on factual knowledge and partly on knowledge of what things are good or bad in themselves, which unlike the former is knowledge of a specifically ethical kind. Thus in order to know what is the right treatment for a particular invalid, we must know both what is likely to be the best medicine for curing him and that he ought to be cured. In this case it is the scientific kind of knowledge which presents the difficulty and not the specifically ethical, but this is by no means always so. We may be hard put to it to decide not only what are the most efficient types of atom bomb, but also when, if ever, we ought to use atom bombs.

This explains how it is that Ethics as a study is not able to give us more help than it does in deciding how we ought to act. To decide this we require not only ethical knowledge but also an empirical knowledge of facts and causal laws, and this is supplied by the sciences or by the common-sense knowledge we all possess of people and physical things. Further, even the specifically ethical element in our knowledge is not capable of complete proof by reasoning but requires an intuitive grasp and valuation of the situation, at which a student of Ethics need not be more competent than another person. The result is that Ethics cannot serve practice in more than an advisory capacity. It cannot decide the issue by itself but can only suggest arguments and considerations that will help us in deciding it. But even this is an important rôle. Because Ethics cannot by itself decide all questions as to what we ought to do, we need not regard it as of no practical value. A person who has studied Ethics should, given goodwill, at least be more likely to look at all relevant sides of an ethical problem, ask the right questions, and avoid elementary confusions. If Ethics could really decide by itself what we ought to do, it would be not only a practical science but the only practical science, and it certainly is not that. It is a great service if it can even only *help* us substantially in deciding what we ought to do. We should add that this must be distinguished from persuading us to do what we know we ought. That is the function of the preacher and orator rather than of the student of Ethics or philosopher.

Some people will start Ethics with the idea that the first function of the study must be to find a definition of its fundamental term, say, good, and that then it will proceed to deduce all manner of conclusions from this definition. Thus Socrates, the first great moral philosopher of Europe, seems to have held that the first and main function of Ethics was to define ethical terms, and questions how we could really be virtuous without knowing the definitions of the virtues. This, however, overlooks a very important possibility. It may well be the case—indeed *prima facie* it looks very much as if it were the case—that the fundamental term or terms of Ethics just cannot be analysed so as to reduce them to anything else and so cannot, in the most important sense of "definition," be defined.[2] The plausibility of such a view is much increased when we

[2] I do not mean to say that there are no senses of "definition" in which the fundamental ethical terms can be defined.

consider what would follow if they all could be defined (otherwise than in terms of each other). They would then be reducible to non-ethical concepts, and Ethics would become just a department of that science to which the non-ethical concepts in question belonged. Thus if "good" were made the fundamental ethical term and defined simply as "what human beings desire" Ethics would become just a branch of psychology, since it is the latter science which studies events and dispositions in mental life such as are covered by the word desire. If it were definable as "what is in accord with the process of natural evolution," Ethics would be just a part of biology; if as "what is conducive to a stable society," part of sociology. Now views of this kind about Ethics have been put forward and will be discussed in a later chapter,[3] but though writers on Ethics differ widely in their attitude to them, there is a fairly general consensus nowadays that they are too simple-minded, and we have no right whatever to assume them at the start. This is borne out by the fact that the methods by which we attain ethical conclusions are very different from those by which the conclusions of any of the three sciences I have just mentioned are attained. Others would start by defining good as "what God wills," but though it may be true that God wills what is good, it does not in the least follow that this is just what "good" means. If it were, Ethics would be part of Theology, and this is again not a plausible view to take. It seems obvious that a person can make ethical judgements without believing in God, and can do so rationally.[4]

It might be thought that we could not advance in Ethics at all if we had not first found out the definitions of the fundamental terms we employ. But this is not the case. For, even if we cannot give a definition of them, we have some idea as to what they mean, otherwise we could not employ them even fairly intelligently, as we do in our ordinary ethical thought, and we have some idea as to when they can be correctly applied. It is the business of

[3] *v.* below Chap. 6.
[4] *v.* below pp. 99-101.

Ethics to start with the imperfect apprehension of the meaning and application of "good," "duty," etc., which we have in daily life and develop it into something better, but it can only do this by studying the ethical judgements we ordinarily make, examining their nature and trying to fit them into that coherent system which, as I have said, is the aim of the thinker. To say that a fundamental ethical term cannot be defined is not to say that we cannot know what it means. It may be indeed that we shall never be able to define it and yet that we may know or come to know very well what it means. And this in two ways and senses of meaning; we may know what the quality, e.g. of goodness is itself by direct experience of it without being able to analyse it, and we may know to what things we may consistently apply the term, and our knowledge in both ways may be capable of improvement without our ever being able to give a precise definition at all. As a matter of fact it can be easily proved that there must be some terms which are indefinable in the sense of not being analysable, reducible to anything else. For if you define A by analysing it in terms of B and C, you must, for the definition to be intelligible, know what B and C are, and though you may analyse B and C also in terms of something else, you cannot go on in this way *ad infinitum*. If you are to analyse your concepts, sooner or later you must come to concepts which are just unanalysable. If so, it will not be a mark of human failure but an inevitable result of the logic of the concepts that we cannot define them. And to say this will be only to say that we cannot reduce them to anything else, not that we cannot know very much about them. Now, if there are any indefinable concepts, concepts as fundamental as good or ought are among those which are most likely to be indefinable. We may be able to say a great deal about them, but that is not to say that we can reduce them without residuum to something else, something not specifically ethical.

Finally, a word about the relation between Ethics and Philosophy. Ethics is commonly classified as a branch of Philosophy because both deal with very general topics transcending the scope of the sciences,[5] but I think it would be a mistake to say that a person cannot study Ethics profitably without also studying the other parts of Philosophy. On the other hand, if he is really interested in the kind of problems with which Ethics deals, it seems to me unlikely that he will be satisfied to stop here and not wish to know something also about general philosophy and the problems which have given rise to Metaphysics (the study of the general nature of the real in so far as this is accessible to human intelligence). If he indulges this desire, he will find that he is helped in dealing with these problems by having studied Ethics and vice versa. Ethics is in fact for most people, I think, the best introduction to Philosophy. The study of both is difficult because it involves a more abstract kind of thinking than any to which we are used in most subjects (other than mathematics) and in ordinary life, but since we are all familiar with ethical problems we shall probably find it much less difficult in that field and had therefore better start by practising there the abstraction required. Also, while to most people most other problems of philosophy seem quite out of touch with ordinary life and the ordinary man's problems, Ethics, if well expounded, can hardly seem so.

It would be unfair to the elementary reader not to stress the fact that Ethics, like other branches of Philosophy, is a subject where very wide differences of opinion exist between competent authorities. The present work does not provide a suitable occasion for expressing my own views in full, but these must inevitably colour my presentation in the following pages, though I have of course tried to give a fair appraisal of those who differ from me. I have indeed hardly said anything, I think, with which at least a very considerable proportion of contemporary philosophers would not be in agreement, but there is no doubt that with much of what I have said a

---

[5] I do not think I can give any more precise definition of philosophy in a few words.

considerable proportion also would disagree. One cannot learn up Ethics (in the philosophical sense), as one can many other subjects, from established authorities with a practical certainty that they are right, even in the main, and certainly what I say should not be accepted by the student until and unless he has worked through the arguments in his own mind and appreciated their point. I need hardly add that my work will not have attained real success if it does not lead him to some further reading on the subject, for which I have at the end[6] given a few suggestions.

[6] v. p. 158.

Chapter 2

Selfishness and Unselfishness

ONE OF THE first questions that presents itself in Ethics is—Why ought I to sacrifice myself for the sake of somebody else? If it is shown to me that some action will have bad consequences for myself, this gives an obvious reason why I should not do it, but it is often felt that it is not so obvious why I should not do what is to my own interest because it has bad consequences for others. Yet every system of ethics has prescribed duties to others as well as to oneself, and no good man is uninfluenced by the prospect of his proposed actions producing bad effects on other men. Confronted with this situation one is tempted to reply by trying to show that the fulfilment of his duties to others is really to the agent's own interests in the long run, either in this life or in another. And some philosophers who ought to have known better, thinking that this can be done, have actually taken the view that ultimately we cannot be under an obligation to pursue anything but our own greatest happiness and that our duties towards others are to be commended solely as efficient, though indirect, means of attaining this happiness. That view is known as egoistic hedonism. "Hedonism" is derived from a Greek word meaning pleasure, and stands for the ethical doctrine that pleasure is the only good, no distinction being ordinarily made by hedonists between "pleasure" and "happiness"; "egoistic" brings out the point that the ultimate aim is *one's own* pleasure. To be fair to the theory we must realize that "pleasure" is intended to cover all satisfactions, not only the mundane pleasures of good dinners and amusements, but the joy of the most selfless and spiritualized love, the unselfish satisfaction of the righteous in furthering the general good, and the delight of the religious mystic in communion with God. Nor does the theory maintain that we should always aim directly at our own pleasure: on the contrary it maintains that we can get pleasure for ourselves best by aiming directly at other things than our own pleasure, particularly the happiness of other men, only it maintains that the sole reason why we ought to aim at the other things is because they are the best means to our own pleasure, not because we are under any obligation to pursue them for their own sake.

The first inclination of most unsophisticated people is to reject egoistic hedonism as blatantly immoral, but even if this turn out to be our final conclusion we must first examine the theory more carefully. And we may feel surprised when we find that such a theory has been held by a number of people of excellent character distinguished for what would normally be described as unselfish devotion to others. This does not indeed prove that the theory is not really in conflict with the most fundamental principles of any tolerable ethics, for a man's practice is often inconsistent with his theory, but it prevents us from dismissing it as mere wickedness or sophistry. And in fact the behaviour that such a theory, consistently carried out, would require of us is not usually by any means so different as one would at first sight expect from the behaviour normally approved ethically. It can easily be shown that under most circumstances the more obvious forms of wrongdoing simply do not pay in happiness even from a completely selfish point of view. Most wicked acts are also highly imprudent, though it is very difficult to get the people who do them to realize this till it is too late. Our happiness is dependent very largely on our relations with other men, and they will be alienated if we are thoroughly unscrupulous and selfish. Happiness also depends very largely on our mind being at peace with itself, and vicious conduct has a very strong tendency to destroy that internal peace. It is a mistake to think of the good as if it were a limited store not capable of increase so that I must inevitably have less if others have more. This is not true even of material wealth, since the common stock may be greatly increased by effort and ingenuity so that there is more to distribute, and since in a commercial exchange both parties commonly benefit. Still less is it true of happiness, which does not depend chiefly on material goods (though a minimum of the latter is necessary). If I acquire more money, it may (though it need not) mean that somebody else will be poorer; but if I gain in happiness through forming more satisfactory relations with others, increasing my ability to appreciate, or becoming more contented with my lot, it will not have the slightest tendency to make anybody else less happy, but rather the reverse. And one of the chief sources of happiness is the consciousness that one is performing a useful function in life and contributing to the welfare of others. The egoist need not deny that we have what are normally called unselfish desires, i.e. desires for the good of others, but he will insist that we gain in happiness ourselves through indulging these desires even more than through indulging the desires which are purely selfish. Bentham, the best known British advocate of the theory I am discussing, was also a great philanthropist, and he was asked whether he was not inconsistent in being so. He replied to the effect that he was not inconsistent, because people took their pleasure in different ways, and he happened to be so constituted that he took his pleasure in philanthropy, whereas another man might, say, take it in drink.

I think, however, that this argument is often pushed too

far. It is by no means possible to show that a man always gains in happiness in proportion to what would generally be regarded as his goodness. Society may punish men for doing wrong, but it can only take cognizance of a small proportion of wrong acts, and suppose society itself is corrupt and punishes people for doing right? It is by no means clear that a good man was at all likely to be happier in Nazi Germany than a bad. Again, in all civilizations of which we know it has been held that it was sometimes a man's duty to risk gravely and even sacrifice his health and life. That is a strange way of acquiring the greatest pleasure possible for the agent! It is not legitimate for the hedonistic egoist to reply that the man will be rewarded in a future life, for even if we grant this we must admit that the only reason for thinking that the action will be rewarded is that we already think it right and admirable, and we cannot, therefore, without committing a vicious circle also hold that the reward makes it right. If our only duty is to pursue our own greatest pleasure, why should we be rewarded for sacrificing our pleasure on this earth to others? *Prima facie* we should be punished. It has often been said that we shall be rendered unhappy by pangs of conscience if we do not sacrifice ourselves for the greater good of others, but we may make a similar reply to this point. Why should we suffer from pangs of conscience if we do not first recognize the action as wrong? And, whilst it may be true of some few people that, if they thought they had saved their own lives by neglecting their duty, they would feel so unhappy about it as to outweigh any pleasure in life, we cannot possibly maintain that this is true of everybody. Surely a man is not excused from the duty to help others because he is so constituted that he can escape the uneasiness about not having helped them by thinking of other things. People's sensitiveness in this matter varies enormously; and when an egoist dwells on the joy of serving others it is difficult to see what he could say if somebody met him with the retort—It is all very well for you, but tastes differ and I am so constituted that I enjoy the selfish pleasures much better than the unselfish.

It seems to me indeed that some of the worst acts ever

done could be justified if egoistic hedonism were true. In Ibsen's play, *The Pretenders,* there is a well-known scene in which the villain lying on his deathbed has an opportunity of avenging himself on an enemy by giving rise to a misapprehension about the succession to the throne, knowing that if he does so he will gratuitously cause a civil war in which thousands will be slain. The situation in the play is complicated by the fear of punishment hereafter, but we have seen this to be irrelevant unless the proposed action can be seen to be wrong independently of the punishment, and in any case we may suppose the man thus tempted to be an atheist. Now if the sole criterion of the rightness or wrongness of an action is its conduciveness to one's own pleasure, I think one would have to say that the act of revenge was right because it would make the last few moments of his life happier than they would otherwise have been. It is true that he would have been likely to be a happier man on the whole if he had not indulged his vindictive desires to such an appalling extent in the past as he must have done to make such an act even a serious temptation, but it is too late for him to alter this now. We could not say to him—Control your vindictive desires now and your character will be improved so that you will be capable of greater pleasure in the future, for he would reply—I have no future. For the egoistic hedonist to make oneself miserable for the good of another man should be positively wicked in the only sense in which anything could be wicked at all.

But, even if the egoistic hedonist could show that his view was compatible with the ordinary canons of morality as regards the external nature of actions, he would still not have justified his position. For it is not only the external act, but the motive which counts in ethics, and the motive he suggests is one which we must regard as essentially unethical. Suppose a man admitted that he only refrains from stealing for fear of being sent to prison, or from ill-treating his children because he has been promised a sum of money if he does not ill-treat them, and we believed him, should we regard him as morally worthy? Not at all, we should condemn him as much or almost as much as if he had been guilty of theft and cruelty, for we should not recognize his motive as a proper one at all. And if so, why should we regard his conduct as any more moral if he refrains from wrong acts in general merely because he is bribed by the prospect of happiness or deterred by the fear of unhappiness whether in this life or in another, even if the happiness or unhappiness is not viewed as coming in such crude ways and as further removed in time? The best we could say is that he shows prudence and far-sightedness, not that he is good. The occasions when we feel markedly under a moral obligation are just *not* the occasions when we are exercised about our own happiness, but the occasions on which we feel an obligation to somebody else that strikes us as such quite independently of whether obedience to it is or is not conducive to our happiness. If a man sacrifices his own happiness needlessly without apparently harming others, the natural word that springs to the lips of the observer in speaking of him is "foolish"; if he sacrifices the happiness of another to further his own apparent happiness, the natural word is not "foolish" but "bad" (in the moral sense of that word). I do not deny that some egoistic hedonists were good men, but I do say that they had a wrong theory of the motives which determined and ought to determine their conduct.

In making these criticisms I have argued from what I called "common-sense ethics," namely, I have appealed to what we cannot help believing in particular ethical situations when we try to look reasonably at the question what one ought to do or approve of doing. If anybody says that all our ethical beliefs are illusions, I must admit that I cannot refute him, only prevent him from refuting me by meeting his arguments, but this completely sceptical position about ethics is one which we may indeed defend in a philosophical argument but not seriously hold in daily life. I note that the people who are most sceptical about the truth of ethical judgements commonly show a righteous moral indignation about at least ethical intolerance, and insist very strongly that we "ought" to seek and accept the truth. And I find it extremely difficult to believe that even the most pronounced ethical sceptic would not be convinced that my actions were bad if he saw me, e.g. wantonly torturing a little child. I shall say something more about the sceptic in a later chapter,[1] but in the meantime we must go on the assumption, which I made in the first chapter, that the ordinary moral judgements which we on reflection cannot help making are the main clue to what is right in Ethics, subject to the test of coherence, and we shall have to ask about each rival theory whether it gives a coherent account of these. I have no hesitation in making the above assumption, and if we do not make it we shall have no Ethics at all, because we shall have no ethical data to organize. Of course this rejection of sheer ethical scepticism is compatible with very much disagreement as to what we do exactly when we make ethical judgements and as to many of the ethical judgements we are called on to make.

However, even complete ethical scepticism should certainly not lead to egoistic hedonism. For even the egoistic hedonist makes some ethical assumptions of a positive kind: he assumes at least that his own pleasure is good in itself, and his pain bad. That this is so he does not and cannot prove. It must therefore be something he sees to be true without proof. And it does seem an obvious enough truth. But in admitting it he has already accepted some ethical convictions without proof just because he sees them to be true, which is what philosophers usually mean by "intuition." Now, if he accepts any at all because he sees them intuitively, ought he not, at least in the absence of positive arguments against them, to accept all those which after careful reflection seem to him intuitively obvious in a like degree? And is it not plain that it is intuitively at least as obvious that it is wrong to do things which hurt others needlessly as that it is wrong unnecessarily to hurt oneself? There are other ethical intuitions incompatible with egoistic hedonism which might be cited, but this one is sufficient. If it is wrong to do things which hurt others for our own amusement, and we see it to be wrong just because it does hurt them, egoistic hedonism is

---

[1] v. below p. 109 ff.

false. For according to egoistic hedonism the only reason why anything is wrong is because it is not conducive to the agent's greatest pleasure. Even if in fact it is the case that it is never conducive to my own greatest pleasure to hurt others, it should be plain that this is not the main reason why it is wrong. If we can see clearly that our own pleasure is good, we can see just as clearly that the fact that an action needlessly and intentionally hurts another is quite sufficient to make it wrong, whether it also hurts me or not. So if we are to be consistent, we must accept both intuitions or neither, unless there are positive arguments which show one to be false, and I do not see what these could possibly be. As a matter of fact it may be doubted whether any important philosophers accept the doctrine of egoistic hedonism to-day, but very many have done so in the past, and it is a view which naturally suggests itself to very many people when they start to think about Ethics, so it is important to settle accounts with it before we move on.

It remains to answer the question how it was that such an obviously mistaken view ever acquired an important influence on ethical thinkers. It seems to me that there were two main reasons for this. In the first place it is plain that the fact that a course of action is conducive to one's own happiness is, as far as it goes, a reason for adopting it. It is a subject for dispute whether this makes it morally obligatory or merely prudent to act in the way proposed, but at least it is a good reason of some sort for doing so. Wantonly to sacrifice one's happiness or incur unhappiness is at least irrational, and that something is rational is a reason for doing it if anything is. Now the project of bringing all Ethics under a single principle so that there is just one kind of circumstance which decides whether an act is right or wrong is very attractive to thinkers, and so when we have found a principle which obviously does give valid reasons for action, there is a temptation to bring all ethical judgements under it. Thinkers have again and again succumbed to such temptations to a premature unification, but knowledge and life are not so simple as that.

Secondly, there is a plausible psychological doctrine

which seemed to support egoistic hedonism. The doctrine, commonly known as *hedonistic psychology*, developed in this way. It is plain that a man can only desire what pleases him. Even if we take the case of the martyr who sacrifices all mundane advantages in order to do what he conceives to be his duty, it may be pointed out that he certainly would not have done this if he had not cared a farthing whether he did his duty or did not. Obviously the thought of doing his duty pleased him or at least the thought of not doing it displeased him. Therefore it was concluded that what he really desired was the pleasure of doing his duty and a similar conclusion was reached as regards every human desire. According to this view what an affectionate mother desires is not her children's happiness but the happiness she will herself get from believing them happy; what the martyr is seeking is not to do his duty or defend his faith, but to avoid the discomfort he would feel at having done that for which his conscience reproached him. In that case the aim of the good and the bad man is the same, their own happiness, only the latter is short-sighted in his views as to what will give him happiness. And since we cannot possibly seek anything else but our own happiness, we cannot be under any obligation to do so. It is only a question whether we seek it wisely or blunder into sacrificing a greater happiness for a lesser.

The people who defined this view in popular argument would have had much excuse if they had been living a hundred years ago, but they do not realize that it is completely rejected by modern psychology, not to say philosophy. To modern psychologists and philosophers it is plain that desire comes on the whole first and pleasure second and that the desire for pleasure as such plays only a small part in life. It is true that I could not desire something that was not in some way pleasant to me (though it might in other respects be very painful), but this does not prove that I only desire anything for the sake of the pleasure it will give. On the contrary in most cases the pleasure is rather the result of the desire than the desire of the anticipation of pleasure. Hedonists say that we avoid doing wrong because we shun the pain of a bad conscience, but should we feel this pain if we had not an aversion to wrongdoing for its own sake? And, though it is perfectly true that a mother almost always feels unhappy herself if her children are unhappy, is this not because she wants her children to be happy for their own sake? It is a mistake to equate even all *selfish* action with action motived by desire for one's own pleasure. Far more evil has been done and on the whole worse traits of character displayed under the influence of the desire for power than under that of the desire for pleasure. We need only think of certain military dictators, to say nothing of the many tyrannical employers, husbands and parents in private life. To seek power for oneself regardless of whether it benefits or harms others is just as selfish as thus to seek pleasure. No doubt the dictators, etc., took pleasure in their power, but that was only because they desired power for its own sake. A thoroughly bad act may be disinterested in the sense of not being aimed at one's own pleasure, as is illustrated by the phrase "disinterested cruelty." If A hates B and gives way to the temptation of hate, what he wants is not his own pleasure but the pain of B, yet of all human actions the worst perhaps are those which show this kind of disinterestedness.

There is a place for the attitude of the egoistic hedonist, since there are many actions, at least when on holiday, where the only or chief relevant point is the amount of pleasure likely to be gained for oneself, but there is nothing specifically moral about it, and unless kept within strict bounds it carries with it a punishment which illustrates the falsity of hedonistic psychology as a general account of human action and desire. It is a well-known truth attested by much experience that, if we seek pleasure too much, it flies, because we are then concentrating our attention on pleasure and not on the objective sources from which alone pleasure can be derived. In order to get pleasure we must be interested in other things besides pleasure for their own sake. Even to enjoy a game we must develop an artificial desire for victory and concentrate our thoughts on this end and not on our pleasure in seeking it. And, while it is legitimate and rational to choose the more pleasant course rather than the less pleasant for oneself where other things are equal, the egoistic hedonist has certainly produced no valid argument against the ordinary view that it is wrong to sacrifice another's greater to one's own lesser pleasure.

But the egoist may resume the contest more plausibly at a higher level. So far I have dealt only with the kind of egoist who will admit only one good, pleasure. But suppose the egoist abandons hedonism and admits that good character or virtue is also an end in itself. He may then argue like this:—I ought always to pursue my own greatest good, for my greatest good is to act virtuously, and I obviously ought always to act virtuously. Even supposing I sacrifice every other personal advantage in order to do my duty, I shall only have sacrificed my lesser good for my greater. If it is argued that this kind of egoism is inconsistent with my duty to help others not only for the sake of my own good but for their own sake, it may be replied that part of virtue just consists in seeking the good of others disinterestedly. It is not only that seeking the good of others is a means to my own but that my own good actually consists partly in seeking theirs. This higher egoism, though rarely found among contemporary philosophers, seems in some form to have been the generally accepted doctrine of classical Greek philosophy, except for those hedonistic philosophers who defended the lower type of egoism which I have already criticized. Thus both Plato and Aristotle base morality on the conception that it is to our own true good to act rightly, though they do not identify good with pleasure but regard the latter as a resultant of the good rather than as constituting it.

A weak point in the egoist's case shows itself when he is asked whether it can ever be a man's duty to sacrifice his life for another. It may be granted that it is very virtuous and therefore a very great good to do so, but can we possibly say that it is such a great good as to outweigh all the goods that the person who sacrificed his life would, if he had continued to live, have attained and enjoyed? Five minutes' or an hour's virtuous action in which he laid down his life could not outweigh the good of years of virtue which he might still have had if he had not made the sacrifice in question. A similar reply may be made if the emphasis is laid not on the goodness displayed in the sacrifice, but on the moral evil of refusing to make it. There is a story of an Irishman who, when he was called a coward for running away in a battle, said—I would rather be a coward for five minutes than a corpse all the rest of my life. I should certainly advise you, if you wish to take up philosophy, to aim at higher standards in respect of logical and accurate expression than did the Irishman, but I think the substance of his objection is such that it is beyond the power of the egoist to answer it. Yet such sacrifice, the conditions for which are by no means limited to battles, is enjoined on occasion and praised in a very high degree by almost every system of ethics.

Further, is it not priggish, and indeed selfish in a bad sense, to make other men a mere means to our own good, even if that good be conceived in its highest and widest sense as the development of our character? Would not a man be a prig rather than a saint if he decided all actions by reference only to their effects on his own character? Nor is it clear that it would always be to the good of others to be treated in this fashion. To take an example, it is a commonplace that power and a rise in the social scale tend to be detrimental to character, yet it by no means follows that a man who realized that he was subject to the temptations which these things bring would be justified in therefore rejecting an important post with a high remuneration, though he had good cause to anticipate it as highly likely that acceptance of it would lead to some deterioration in his own morality. What should we have thought if Churchill or some member of his cabinet had brought forward these objections against holding office in 1940, thus subordinating the nation's welfare to the good of his own character?

An important modern philosopher, Professor G. E. Moore, has tried to show egoism to be self-contradictory.[2] He was thinking mainly of egoistic hedonism, but the same argument, if valid at all, would, as he recognizes, apply to

---

[2] *Principia Ethica* p. 98 ff.

any theory which held it a man's sole duty to pursue his own good, whether this good was conceived more widely or identified with pleasure. Moore argued that the egoistic hedonist is committed to maintaining that his own pleasure is the only good there is. Now, if this is so, the same would apply equally to you and me and every one of the two thousand or so million inhabitants of the earth, so there follows from his view the completely absurd conclusion that every one of over two thousand million things is the one and only thing good-in-itself, than which you could hardly have a conclusion more self-contradictory. Obviously the same objection would, if valid at all, apply to whatever we regarded as good, provided we took the egoistic point of view. It would be just as self-contradictory to say of every man's virtue that it was the only good as it would be to say it of every man's pleasure. But I think the egoist (and even the egoistic hedonist) has a reply which will enable him to escape the charge of actual self-contradiction. The usual view of the egoist is surely not that each man's own good is the only good, but that it is the only good at which he is under any obligation to aim. Other people's goods would on his view be equally good, only they would not impose on him any obligation to further them for their own sake. The position appears self-contradictory only if it is assumed that it is our duty to produce the greatest good, to whomever the good belongs, and this assumption, though highly plausible, is not absolutely necessary. We may be under an obligation to produce some good things and not others, and the egoist is maintaining that the only good things which we are under an obligation to produce are those which will belong to ourselves.

But, although there is no actual self-contradiction in the egoist position, a similar argument may be used to make it appear at least very unplausible. For, granted the amount of good be the same, why on earth should the mere fact that it belongs not to me but to someone else exempt me from all obligation in regard to it? It is not as if the sense of obligation were specially connected with *our* good. On the contrary it seems to be an essential feature of the developed moral sense that it aims at being impartial between oneself and others, and forbids us to treat a good as more important because it is our own good. This being so, it seems hard indeed to maintain that we are under a paramount obligation to develop goodness in ourselves but have no direct obligation whatever to further it in other men. This is not to say that we should always be setting out directly to improve the morals of other people, a policy which, if not very carefully carried out, may easily defeat its own ends, though on the other hand it would be a gross exaggeration to deny that one man can very often help another to be morally better.

In sharp contrast to even the higher egoism and still more to egoistic hedonism the ethical view popularly preached in Christian countries has usually been that the primary virtue is unselfishness viewed as the readiness to sacrifice oneself for other men. But this view cannot, any more than egoistic hedonism, be carried to its absolute extreme. A society in which everybody spent his life sacrificing all his pleasure for others would be even more absurd than a society whose members all lived by taking in each other's washing. In a society of such completely unselfish people who would be prepared to accept and benefit by the sacrifice? And the purposeless surrender of one's happiness is mere folly. This suggests the view that self-sacrifice is only required or indeed justified where it is necessary in order to secure for somebody else a *greater* good than that sacrificed, for otherwise (except in the rare case where the good sacrificed and the good gained are exactly equal) there is a net loss of good on the whole, which is undesirable. But it is not practicable to measure happiness with such mathematical exactitude, and the good man will not grudge it if he loses a little more than the man he benefits gains or count his own sacrifices so carefully. That would be niggardliness rather than generosity. Further, since most people are more likely to be too selfish than too unselfish, it is generally better, if in doubt, to risk going too far rather than too short a way in the direction of sacrifice. But the other error is possible, and not very uncommon. If committed out of genuine kindness it is a highly pardonable error and usually results in no harm except a slight loss of pleasure, but the motives are often rather more dubious, e.g. desire for power, desire to feel "what a good person I am," sexual desire more or less perverted. Psychologists have pointed out a "masochistic" tendency in many people which leads them to unnecessary and harmful sacrifices for particular individuals, which is of course quite compatible with general selfishness towards others. Further, whatever the motive of the sacrifice, we must take account not only of the loss of pleasure by the benefactor, which may be easily compensated by satisfaction in the act, direct or indirect, but of the effect on the character of the beneficiary. It can hardly be good for a person to be the constant recipient of unreasonable sacrifices, and is likely to make him selfish and exigent. Yet there is nothing that calls for greater admiration than devoted and cheerful sacrifice of great goods or incurring of great hardships where it is really called for if another person is to be saved from unhappiness. And even if we think that the sacrifice will be rewarded by greater happiness for the agent in this life or another, we cannot make this desire of reward the motive without gravely spoiling the spirit of the action.

We cannot therefore define an unselfish man as one who sacrifices his welfare to others, but only as one who does so within reason. We ought not to treat either other people as a mere means to our own happiness or ourselves as a mere means to the happiness of others. The point is that the interests of others should be treated on just the same level as one's own, so that the antithesis between self and others is made as little prominent in one's ethical thinking as possible. It is impossible even for the best man to feel the misfortunes of others as much as his own (except for a very few individuals of whom he is specially fond), and if he did he would be crushed by the misery in the world to and beyond the point of complete mental collapse, but it is still possible to treat their misfortunes as equally important. The principle "Do unto others as you would be done by," cannot indeed be applied literally, because people wish different things, and because it is not always right to give people what they wish, e.g. I might wish not to be punished when punishment was deserved and right. But it serves epigrammatically to express the impartiality towards ourselves and others at which we ought to aim in ethics, though we shall sometimes have to consider rather what men ought to wish than what they actually do wish. All this suggests another theory of Ethics, which has been widely held, namely the theory that what we ought to do is to seek to promote the greatest happiness, not only of ourselves, but of people in general. This theory I shall discuss in the next chapter.

Chapter 3

The Pursuit of the General Happiness

IF PLEASURE or happiness is the only thing good-in-itself —and it is certainly the only thing about the *intrinsic* goodness of which there is anything like universal agreement—it seems irrational to hold that it makes any difference to its goodness who enjoys the happiness. And it seems reasonable to hold that it is our duty to produce as much good as possible and that it is wrong to neglect any opportunities to do so. From these assumptions we get a form of hedonism which differs from the egoistic form and seems to approach much more closely to what we ordinarily believe about ethical matters. The theory is most commonly known by the name of *Utilitarianism*. It is also sometimes called *Universalistic Hedonism*, "universalistic" because it considers everybody's good, and "hedonism" because it holds pleasure to be the only good. It maintains that our sole duty is to produce as much pleasure as possible, counting for this purpose a diminution of pain as equivalent to an increase in pleasure, and holds that in doing so we should count every man's pleasure as of equal worth to that of any other man. (It makes no distinction, any more than does egoistic hedonism, between happiness and pleasure, happiness being regarded as prolonged pleasure.) It thus agrees with egoistic hedonism as to what is good, but not as to what are the ultimate principles of ethical action. Both theories hold that pleasure is the only good, but while egoistic hedonism thinks we are under no obligation to further the happiness of anybody else except as a means to our own, the theory I am now going to discuss maintains that we are under a direct obligation to pursue happiness as such, to whomever the happiness belongs. The theory is now held by very few moral philosophers, but it was extremely important in the nineteenth and in a less fully thought-out form in the eighteenth century, and is no doubt approximately the working theory of vast numbers of people to-day in so far as they can be said to have an ethical theory at all. Its most important exponents in this country were John Stuart Mill[1] and Sidgwick.[2]

Now it is quite obvious that the amount of happiness or pain produced by our actions should be at least one of the chief criteria for deciding which actions we ought to perform. There are vast numbers of actions which are wrong for no other reason than that they tend to produce pain or unhappiness in other people, and if it can be shown that an act will lead to suffering, this is, usually at least, quite a sufficient reason why we ought not to perform it. Further, a utilitarian can deal with most of the relatively rare cases where it is right to inflict pain by contending that the infliction of pain now is necessary to avoid greater pain in the future or as a means to a gain in happiness which is worth the cost. We must remember, as with egoistic hedonism, that under "pleasure" are meant to be comprised all satisfactions and joys and not only the relatively "lower" ones to which the term pleasure is most commonly applied in ordinary speech. We must further realize that the utilitarian is not bound to suppose that in

[1] *Utilitarianism* (1861).
[2] *The Methods of Ethics* (1874).

practice we ought always to settle what we are to do by a direct calculation of the amount of pleasure likely to be produced. He usually insists on the contrary that there are certain rules of behaviour such as those against lying and stealing whose violation human experience has adequately shown to be productive of unhappiness, and that in consequence we do not need to calculate afresh each time the amount of happiness or unhappiness likely to be produced before deciding to obey one of these laws. The ultimate ground for their validity lies in the general happiness, but we need not go back to this ultimate ground each time, any more than we need before applying an established mathematical law go back each time to the axioms on which it is based. Nor can utilitarianism possibly be dismissed as selfish, for it bids us treat the happiness or pain of any other man as no less important than our own. And utilitarianism has the great attraction of being a relatively simple theory and one in close relation to verifiable empirical facts. For an Ethics which admits only one good will obviously be simpler to apply than one which admits several that may on occasion conflict, and pleasure and pain are after all feelings the occurrence of which we can easily verify in a straightforward empirical way. All this does not however prove it to be the true theory.

As compared to common-sense morality a consistent utilitarianism would be in some respects stricter and in others less strict. Ordinarily we consider that we are much more under an obligation to some people than to others. We admit indeed that we are under some obligation to help anyone in need, but we feel a very much stronger obligation to promote the happiness of our own family, as is shown by the general attitude to appeals for charity. It is clear that the money spent by a man in order to provide his son with a university education could save the lives of many people who were perishing of hunger in a famine, yet most people would rather blame than praise a man who should deprive his son of a university education on this account. Further, while the obligation to contribute something to charity if one can afford it is generally recognized, only a very small minority of people have felt it their duty to curtail their comforts and luxuries very seriously on that account, and still less the comforts and luxuries of those dependent on them. Yet there can hardly be any doubt that, even if we allow for any indirect evil effects which might accrue, in most cases money given to any even tolerably well managed charity will do much more good by relieving the suffering of those in distress than would be done by using the same money to increase the pleasure of a person who is at all tolerably comfortable by enabling him to have a more pleasant house, better furniture, more tobacco, more holiday travel, etc. This does not, however, straightway prove the utilitarian wrong. He may reply that all but the very poor ought to give much more money to charity than on the average they do, and in view of the very small proportion of the national income that is spent on this and the vast amount of suffering in the world which calls for help, it seems to me plain that he is so far right. But, even if we grant this, it still seems plain to me, and I am sure would seem so to almost everybody else that, if a man were to deprive his wife and children against their will of all comforts and purchasable pleasures, leaving them only bare necessaries, on the ground that he could use the money thus saved to preserve several families from a greater pain or loss of happiness than he inflicted on his own by giving it to a charitable organization he would be acting wrongly not rightly. Again, suppose he obtained the money to give to the charity by stealing it from a man very much richer than himself. He might argue that the victim of his theft would lose little in happiness by being a few pounds worse off, while the people to whom he gave the money would be saved from great misery. Even if he kept the money himself, he might indeed argue that, being much poorer,[3] he would gain more in happiness from it than the other

---

[3] Note that I am referring to theft by a man who is comparatively poor, not by one who is starving, still less one whose family is starving. I am not prepared to say that it is wrong for such people to steal in a community where there are no other means such as poor relief available to save them from their desperate condition.

man lost. These reflections seem to disclose a sharp conflict between utilitarianism and even enlightened commonsense morality. According to the former there is an equal obligation to further the happiness of everybody, according to the latter we have special obligations to some people much stronger than those we have to others; according to the former what produces most happiness is always right, according to the latter it is wrong to produce happiness by stealing and lying.

The utilitarian however will contend that the conflict is not a real but only an apparent one. He will argue that, if we take a more far-sighted view, we can see that greater happiness is produced by recognizing and insisting on special obligations. Family life is a great source of happiness, and family life as we know it would be impossible if we did not look on ourselves as having much stronger obligations to members of our family than to perfect strangers. And, if we admitted the principle that the poor were ethically entitled to steal from the rich, the result would be a social confusion which would be far worse than the present system. But it seems to me that what the utilitarian has done here is to point out that a whole class of acts or system of recognized obligations produces good results in the way of happiness, not that each particular act does so. We may admit that it would be a bad thing if the poorer generally and indiscriminately tried to steal from the richer, but does it necessarily follow from this that to do so in any one instance is wrong? A poor man who is prepared to cheat a richer may say—It would be a bad thing if everybody acted like me, but why should not I do so, when it is certain that my action will not result in every body acting like me? It seems only possible to answer such a question adequately if we say that it is *unfair* to profit by the rules governing society and yet refuse yourself to obey them. But if we appeal to fairness, we are introducing another consideration besides happiness. It may therefore be doubted whether we can give an adequate account of our obligations without abandoning utilitarianism and admitting that there are other obligations which we should not ignore even in order to produce greater happiness and that it is bad to acquire happiness by unfair means whether for ourselves or others. It is indeed difficult to maintain that it cannot under any circumstances be right to lie, etc., on utilitarian grounds, e.g. to save life, but it seems to me pretty clear that utilitarian principles, logically carried out, would result in far more cheating, lying and unfair action than any good man would tolerate. This is not of course the same thing as saying that utilitarians are more likely to cheat and lie than other people, but only that if they carried out their theory consistently they would be so.

We may add that utilitarianism is far from being so simple a theory to apply as has been claimed by its advocates. How are we going to measure against each other quite different kinds of pleasure and say how many times more pleasure seeing *Hamlet* will give a particular man than will a good dinner? And it becomes still more complicated when we introduce different agents who cannot be expected all to take the same amount of enjoyment in the same pleasures. Yet such calculations are necessary if we are to apply the utilitarian criterion consistently to all practical questions. Similar difficulties will no doubt arise with any ethical theory that takes account of consequences, as we surely must, but at least this shows that utilitarianism has less cause than might be thought to pride itelf on its simplicity. It is about as difficult to estimate the relative pleasantness of different pleasures as it would be on a non-hedonistic view to estimate their relative goodness.

It is however very hard to give any conclusive disproof of utilitarianism by considering the kind of actions to which it would logically lead. For suppose I argue that utilitarianism is a mistaken theory because, if carried out consistently, it would require me in a given situation to do something which is wrong. Now in any actual instance of a kind that could provide a ground for dispute the effects will be very complicated and uncertain, so that will always leave a loophole for the utilitarian to argue that I am wrong in my views as to their bearing on general happiness and that the act which seems right to common sense is really after all on a long view that most productive of happiness. And even if there are some instances where this is very unplausible (as indeed I think there are), he may reply by amending common-sense ethics here and saying that the act we ordinarily think right in this case is not really so. We are not bound to and indeed cannot accept the common sense view (where there is one) about every action. The utilitarian view could only be shaken by a very considerable series of such instances. As I have suggested already, I think that it can be shaken by citing a series of instances of cheating and lying where what a good man could not help regarding as a "dirty trick" seemed to add to the general happiness, but it is easier to attack utilitarianism by considering its bearing not on the question what we ought to do but rather on the question what is good in itself.

Now the answer of utilitarianism to this question is very simple. The only thing good in itself, it maintains, is pleasure. But there are all kinds of pleasures, and it is very difficult to regard them as all of equal value. To take an instance given by G. E. Moore,[4] a man who is watching a Shakespearian tragedy with full understanding and aesthetic appreciation at its highest pitch may be enjoying no more pleasure quantitatively than a drunkard who is amusing himself by smashing crockery, yet it is surely obvious that the former's pleasure is worth more than the latter's. But, if it is, there must be other factors besides pleasure on which the goodness of an experience depends, since the pleasure is *ex hypothesi* not greater in the former case than it is in the latter but only qualitatively better. Mill[5] tried indeed to reconcile his utilitarianism with the admission that a lesser pleasure might rationally be preferred to a greater on the ground of the superior quality of the former, but it is generally, and I think rightly, agreed among philosophers that he failed to escape inconsistency. To say that pleasure is the only good and yet admit that a lesser pleasure may be preferable to a greater is like saying

[4] *Ethics*, p. 147.
[5] *Utilitarianism*, Chap. II.

that money is the only thing which counts and then adding that money earned by public work is better than the same amount of money earned by business. If pleasure is the only good, the more pleasure always the better.

In order to decide whether one pleasure can be qualitatively better than another let us consider the following instances. Let us suppose that you were offered fifty more years, each equal in quantity of pleasure to the most pleasant year you have ever spent, but that the pleasure was to be derived entirely from eating, drinking, playing childish games and lying in the sun. Imagine this proposed life shorn of every element of intelligence above that of an imbecile, of all aesthetic experience, of all love of other men. Now suppose that you were offered as an alternative forty-nine years of equal pleasure, but that in this case the pleasure was no longer to be derived exclusively from these sources but also from the exercise of intelligence, of love, and of a developed capacity to appreciate the best in art and literature, and suppose also that the effect of the two alternative lives on the general happiness would be equal, the superior advantages for other men that one would expect to accrue from the second life being neutralized and only just neutralized by some evil influence that would intervene if you chose the second and not if you chose the first. Can we doubt that it would be better to choose the second? Yet, if utilitarianism were true, it would certainly be better to choose the first since you would thereby obtain a year's more pleasure. The utilitarian may reply that you would soon get bored by the first life and not enjoy it, but suppose some drug or conditioning process were invented that would prevent you getting bored so that you really got the pleasure promised? It is not inconceivable that a drug might be invented which had these properties. To take a slightly less fanciful illustration, I think Huxley's *Brave New World* is a good refutation of hedonism because it shows us an imaginary state of society which is hedonistically most satisfactory and yet ethically revolting.

Suppose again two communities in which an equal amount of pleasure was enjoyed and an equal amount of pain suffered. But suppose that in one community the citizens were selfish, unjust and capable only of pleasures which did not involve considerable intelligence, aesthetic appreciation, goodness or love, and that in the other community they derived their pleasures chiefly from those sources which I have just excluded from the first. Surely it is plain that the state of the second community would be much better than the state of the first. Yet, if utilitarianism were true, the two states should be equal in value. Two objections may be made against this example. First, it may be objected that the qualities possessed by the members of the second community would of their inherent nature necessarily lead to a greater happiness than any possessed by the first. But we can meet this by supposing the second community to be much less advantageously situated than the first as regards wealth, health and external circumstances. These factors might quite conceivably counteract the advantages in respect of happiness which would otherwise accrue to them from their superior character. Secondly, it may be objected that we cannot measure happiness as exactly as these examples presuppose. To this we may reply by substituting "approximately equal" or "equal as far as we can tell" for "exactly equal." If we are not able to compare experiences in respect of pleasure, utilitarianism cannot be applied at all; and if we can compare them, there is a good sense in saying that two lives or two communities are "equal in happiness as far as we can tell," meaning that we have no reason to think either happier than the other. That is all that is needed for my illustrations, and this negative condition certainly may be fulfilled.

Thirdly, let us suppose a man revelling in the infliction of tortures on his enemy. Of course this will be very painful for his victim and may have other less direct detrimental consequences in the future for the general welfare, but we are not now asking whether this state of affairs is conducive to the general good, we are asking about its value or disvalue in itself. Let us just consider the state of mind of the man inflicting the suffering. He is enjoying himself, yet can we say that his state of mind is good in itself? Surely it is on the contrary very bad indeed, and the more so the greater the pleasure. As a matter of fact his state of mind would still be very bad if he were not really inflicting the pain but only thought he was, like a witch-doctor who believed he could make his enemy suffer by roasting his effigy over a slow fire, yet in this case his victim would suffer no pain at all. But, if utilitarianism were true, the state should be good in itself because pleasurable, however deplorable its effects. Still less could it be the case on the utilitarian view that the state was made worse, not better, by increasing the pleasure.

Let us now take other instances which show up the defects of the utilitarian theory. Suppose a shipwreck in which two men are left clinging to a raft unable to support more than one. Let us call them A and B. Now suppose A to be a person whose life is of much less value to society or other individuals than that of B. Under these circumstances we should hold it a very meritorious act of A to surrender his place to B, but we should hold it the reverse of meritorious on the part of B to push off A. Yet the effect of the two acts would be almost the same: by either the life of A is sacrificed and that of B preserved. The only important difference in the effects seems to be that in the second case B will, if he is fundamentally good, be troubled by remorse, and if he is not so troubled, will probably deteriorate in character still further as the result of his action. But this cannot possibly be cited as a reason for the different estimate of the two actions, since unless it is already admitted that the second act is wrong there is no point in the remorse. Of course the utilitarian may argue that we are mistaken in thinking the second act wrong, it B is entitled to be certain that his life is really more important, and that the only reason why we think it wrong is because it would be a dangerous principle in general to allow a man to be judge whether his life was or was not more useful than that of another man. But the very most the utilitarian could maintain with the least show of plausibility would be that the action of B was excusable or not blameworthy, he could not possibly maintain that it was positively admirable, yet we should all admit that the action of A which had practically the same effects was not just excusable but positively admirable. Utilitarianism cannot account for this difference. The latter cannot be explained by effects on happiness but only by something intrinsically good in the nature of the one action. It is not a matter of pleasurable feelings—A probably did not enjoy drowning—but of something quite different from pleasure.

Finally, utilitarianism may be condemned as irreconcilable with the dictates of justice. The principle of utilitarianism tells us only to produce as much happiness as possible, thus implying that the way in which it is distributed does not matter. But justice requires that of two distributions which produce equal happiness we ought to prefer the fairer to the less fair, and that we ought to do this even if slightly less happiness is yielded by the former than by the latter. To take an extreme instance, suppose we could slightly increase the collective happiness of ten men by taking away all happiness from one of them, would it be right to do so? It is perhaps arguable that it would if the difference in happiness of the nine was very large, but not if it was very slight. And if the happiness of the nine were purchased by the actual torture of the one, the injustice of it would seem to poison the happiness and render it worse than valueless even if they were callous enough to enjoy it. Yet on the utilitarian view any distribution of good, however unfair, ought to be preferred to any other, however just, if it would yield *the slightest* additional happiness. Again, ought an innocent man to be punished, if it would on the balance cause less pain with an equal deterrent effect to punish him than it would to punish the guilty? In view of these difficulties it is not surprising that to-day very few philosophers could be found to accept utilitarianism.

What modifications must be made in utilitarianism in order to deal with these examples satisfactorily? In the first place we must admit that not only the quantity but the quality of a pleasure is relevant, so that a lesser pleasure of a higher kind may rightly be preferred to a greater pleasure of a kind which is lower. But what makes one pleasure higher than another? It is not a difference in the nature of the pleasurable feeling as such. It is rather a difference in the activity of the mind with which it is connected or in its object. Some pleasures are regarded as higher than others, because they are connected with thinking, aesthetic experiences, love, moral action, and we regard these activities as higher than eating and drinking and as having an intrinsic value which must be added to any intrinsic value possessed by the pleasures they give as pleasure. Now, if we classify pleasures and activities according to their object, we value specially those concerned with the pursuit of truth, beauty and goodness. As regards the last, my example of the shipwreck has brought out the point that certain morally good acts of self-sacrifice have an intrinsic value not dependent on any pleasant feelings they produce, and my example of the man torturing his enemy has brought out the point that moral badness and not only pain is intrinsically evil. Most people who have thought about the subject have attributed an ultimate value to these three—truth, beauty and goodness (or rather the search for and attainment of them), as well as to love between human beings and (with the religious) to what they call contemplation of or communion with God.

Finally, the point that of two distributions of the same amount of happiness the fairer should be preferred to the unfair seems to show that not only the amount of good distributed but the way in which it is distributed can be intrinsically good (or evil). It is not possible indeed to *prove* that any of these things are good-in-themselves, but neither is it possible to prove that this is so with pleasure. As I have said, the utilitarian has to admit that he can know without proof that pleasure is good-in-itself. Cannot we equally see that these other things are so? Pleasure is only the good of one side of our nature, the feeling side; but we are not only feeling, we are also thinking and acting beings. If so, why should the good of our feeling side be the only one that is of value as an end in itself and not merely as a means to something else?

The utilitarian is indeed right in holding that whatever is good is pleasant. Even painful acts of self-sacrifice done because they are right or out of love give a certain amount of satisfaction to the person who does them, though this may easily be quite outweighed for him at the time by the suffering involved. But the utilitarian is still wrong in holding that what is good is so only because it is pleasurable. Although all good things are pleasant, their goodness is not in proportion to their pleasantness, and more often something is pleasant because it is good than good because it is pleasant. Yet a very large proportion of the ethical questions with which we are confronted can legitimately be answered by applying the utilitarian criterion. And this for two reasons. In the first place there are many cases of action where there simply are no relevant considerations but the pleasure or pain produced, since other values do not come in question in these particular cases. A sick man's virtue may be more important than his freedom from pain, but since he may just as well be virtuous if he is healthy, a doctor may usually freely prescribe for the latter without considering the former. A vast number of wrong actions are pronounced wrong simply because they give pain, and probably a large majority of actions pronounced good are so because they give pleasure or alleviate pain and are done on that account. Secondly, it is plain that actions which promote the other values, knowledge, beauty, love, virtue, justice, will also on the whole make for happiness. This explains why the utilitarian criterion is not so wildly off the mark that it is impossible for intelligent men to be deceived into accepting it as the only ultimate criterion in ethics.

It is of interest that utilitarianism made its mark especially in the field of political and large scale social reform. In these matters I think utilitarianism comes very much nearer to providing a completely satisfactory criterion than in the sphere of individual ethics. For here we are concerned rather with the removal of causes of unhappiness than with the direct promotion of positive good. You cannot produce high morality or fine art or science by law or make people love each other, and you had much better not try, but you can ameliorate their physical state and remove many causes of avoidable suffering. We must not regard it as an argument for utilitarianism that, if it were universally adopted and consistently carried out by everybody, we should be secure from war and soon end acute poverty throughout the world, for the same would be true of any at all plausible ethical theory, of which there are a great variety. But I wish for more straightforward utilitarian argument in politics, not less. I should like to emphasize this point strongly because, whatever is the ultimate truth about utilitarianism, it is plain at least that we have no right to increase greatly human unhappiness or subtract greatly from human happiness, unless this grave disadvantage be outweighed by a very important gain in respect of other goods, or could only be avoided by action that for some other reason was immoral (contingencies which do not seem to me at all likely). Now I shall not go into this point at length because I am not writing a book on Politics, but I am convinced that a careful survey of either Communism, Fascism, Nazism or *Laissez-faire* Individualism would show that they have made enormous sacrifices of human happiness which were not necessary to further any good that could rationally be approved by a sane man or to avoid action that could be called immoral. Hence they must be condemned even apart from the fact that they are of the greatest detriment also to goods other than happiness.

Chapter 4

Duty for Duty's Sake

HAVING EXAMINED THEORIES which based ethics on happiness, it is well to turn to the other extreme and take the theory of the great German philosopher Kant (1724–1803). His ethics was to a large extent motived by a reaction against hedonism, especially the egoistic variety of it, and his theory took the form that the primary thing to consider is not the happiness or unhappiness produced by an action, or indeed any of its consequences, but the nature of the action itself. Central to his ethics is the concept of the *good will*. By this he means not good will in the sense of kindly feeling, but the doing one's duty because it is one's duty, or as he put it, "out of respect for the moral law." He begins his ethics by declaring that this good will is the only thing which can be held to be unconditionally good, and he insists again and again on its supreme and incomparable worth, which it retains even if unable to achieve any of the external results valued and desired by us. There is something splendid about a self-sacrificing and distinterested act, even if through no fault of the agent it fails entirely. Kant does not indeed deny all value to happiness, but he maintains that happiness (which he like the ultilitarians equates with pleasure) is only conditionally good. By this he means that, if we have the good will, it is good that we should also be happy, but not otherwise. This is not to say happiness is only good as a means: for if a person has the good will, it is better that he should also be happy, even apart from any future consequences of his happiness. But it is to say that happiness, unlike the good will, is not good under all circumstances but only under some, namely, in the presence of the good will. Kant never suggests that anything else besides the good will and happiness can be intrinsically good and, strange to say, it seems that he valued knowledge, love, and all qualities of the mind other than the good will merely as means. Nor does he like Mill draw any distinction in quality between pleasures, but treats all pleasures and all desires as on the same level, as being neither good nor bad but ethically indifferent. His main contribution to ethics was to develop the idea of duty for duty's sake which previous moralists had usually neglected. Of the other things generally accounted as values he says little.

In developing his concept of dutiful action Kant insists on a very important distinction he draws between hypothetical and categorical imperatives. A hypothetical imperative tells us to act in a certain way because it will tend to produce a certain result, and the need for the action is thus conditional on our desiring the result in question; but a categorical imperative commands us unconditionally. For example, "take such and such a road if you want to go to London" (which you may not do) is a hypothetical imperative; "do not tell lies" a categorical. Categorical imperatives alone, he holds, are ethical. Obedience to them is a duty, while obedience to hypothetical imperatives is at the best prudential. But what is the motive for obeying categorical imperatives? It is not a desire for some future result of the action, whether for ourselves or even others, otherwise they would be hypothetical; it is the motive to do the right as such, *respect for the moral law,* which Kant regards as essentially different from desire, though it can like desire serve as a motive for action. Kant further draws a very sharp distinction between actions which are outwardly in accordance with the moral law but really motivated by self-interest and actions which are done from a sense of duty. The first kind of action may be externally the same as the second, but this does not give it any inner worth whatever. We cannot praise a tradesman for his honesty if he is honest merely because he thinks it good business policy.

A difficulty that strikes most readers of Kant is that men seem often to perform the most noble and self-sacrificing actions under the influence of love rather than out of a conscious sense of duty, and it seems unfair to deny all intrinsic value to such actions. We should actually think better of a father who did his duty to his children from love without thinking of it as a duty than we should of one who felt no love for his children but without desiring to benefit them did his duty to them just because it was his duty. Commentators are not agreed exactly how far Kant lays himself open to this criticism, but according to the interpretation which I am on the whole inclined to favour he did not commit himself to the view that a person's action had no moral value if it was motived both by some desire and by respect for the moral law in such a way that either motive by itself would have been sufficient to bring about the act, but only to the view that it had no moral value if it was motived entirely by desire. In that case at any rate he has a reasonable defence. He might urge that any desire, however fine in itself, may lead us to act wrongly, and therefore, if we let ourselves be guided solely by it, we are risking doing wrong, and cannot lay claim to any merit even if by good luck we are right. It is obvious that the love of any one individual or group of individuals may lead us to further their interests at the expense of others or in ways which are normally wicked. We may disagree with Kant and ascribe intrinsic value to some forms of love and some desires other than respect for the moral law, but at any rate we cannot ascribe to them or to action motived solely by them the particular *kind* of value known as moral value which Kant has so effectively brought to our notice. On the other hand we must recognize that the supreme ethical motive which Kant felt as respect for an abstract law is felt by others as an urge to pursue the supreme good for humanity, and by others still as the love of God. We must not of course condemn as unethical anyone who does not envisage it in just Kant's way.

Now let us consider the application of Kant's theory to the chief question of Ethics, namely, what acts are right and why are they right. He was debarred by his principles from answering this question simply by a straightforward reference to their consequences. For to make consequences decisive is to base the rightness or wrongness of an action on the good or evil it produces. Now the only goods Kant recognized were, as we have seen, the good will and happiness. The former is a matter of the action and its motives and not of the consequences at all, and the latter could not be made the supreme criterion of what is right without adopting utilitarianism, a view with which Kant had no sympathy. He was therefore constrained to look for a means of explaining why some actions are right and some wrong otherwise than by reference to consequences.

He had another reason for this attitude. In philosophy one of the most fundamental distinctions is that between empirical knowledge, or knowledge based on observation, and *a priori* knowledge, or knowledge based on pure thought and reasoning, as in mathematics. Now Kant was convinced that ethical knowledge is *a priori* and not empirical. Observation can only tell us what is, and you cannot derive what ought to be from what is, he argued, and he also thought that ethical principles have a necessity which cannot find a place in the merely empirical world. He concluded that the general principles of Ethics like those of mathematics were discoverable *a priori* by thinking and not by generalization from experience, though of course they have to be applied to empirical facts, as indeed are the principles of mathematics. For instance, he held we could know *a priori* that we ought not to tell lies, though we obviously need empirical knowledge to decide what is the true thing to say and how best to say it so as to make ourselves understood by others.

How are the principles of Ethics then to be established? *A priori* conclusions are commonly proved in other fields of thought by showing that there would be a contradiction in denying them, and Kant tried to apply this method to Ethics. Thus he argued that it is wrong to tell lies because, if everybody lied whenever he thought it suited him, the lies would not be believed and would therefore lose all point and be self-defeating. Kant regards this as showing universal lying to be logically impossible, but he does not think it can be shown of all wrong ethical principles that their universal application would be impossible, but merely that it would contradict our nature to will it. Thus in discussing why we ought to help other men who are in need he says that society could still subsist if the principle of not helping others in need were universalized, but we could not consistently will it universalized because there are many possible circumstances in which we should wish to be helped ourselves. This sounds as if Kant were after all falling back on an egoistic motive, but I do not think it is really so. Kant's point is not—Give to others so that they may give to you in return, but—It is not consistent, we might put it "not fair," to benefit by the kindness of others, as you must, and yet refuse to do others a kindness when they need it. While the former motive is prudential, the latter is certainly moral. Kant's general principle is —"Act as if the maxim of your action were to become by your will law universal." When we act according to a principle which we could not wish to be generally applied, Kant thinks we are acting immorally.

Kant here has clearly hold of something very important, though the detailed applications he makes of his principle are harder to defend. Let us see what plain ethical truths we can learn from him. In the first place, it is significant that what the man who does wrong believing it to be wrong usually wishes is by no means that everybody should act in the way he proposes to do. The thief is the last person who would wish others to steal from him. What the bad man wishes in general is not that the rule he breaks should cease to hold, but that an exception should be made to it in his own favour. It is this arbitrary making of exceptions in one's own interest which is essentially immoral, Kant is saying. Secondly, it does seem that in some cases the use of a criterion like Kant's is more in accord with our ordinary ethical thinking than is straightforward utilitarianism. There are cases where the harm a particular action does is insignificant but we condemn it because it is one of a class of actions. Thus, if I tried to evade taxation and argued that I was under no obligation to pay my taxes because the loss of that amount of money would make no appreciable difference to the functioning of the State but made a considerable difference to me, the usual answer would be to ask in return— What would happen if everybody acted like that? But it should be noted that, while it is a common test of the rightness or wrongness of an action to ask what would happen if everybody acted in that way, what the person who asks has in mind is usually the good or bad consequences that would accrue if everyone so acted, while Kant claimed to base the obligatoriness of his laws not on the harm their general breach would do but on the supposition that there would be some kind of contradiction in a general defiance of them, since universal breach of a law would take away the point in breaking it. Thirdly, it is true that there is really something inconsistent about wickedness in the sense that it aims at an end the attainment of which is at the same time by its inherent nature self-defeating. For the man who is guilty of it seeks satisfaction for himself, yet real satisfaction cannot be attained by evil but only by good. This was perhaps the main point made by both Plato and Hegel in Ethics.

Finally, we must admit that all our answers to the question what is right are of universal application in the sense that, granted an act is right for me, it must be right under the same conditions for everybody. In this sense any moral decision claims universality. Only we should in some cases have to include among the conditions to be taken into account not only external circumstances but differences of individual psychology. It does not follow that, because it was right for Kant to engage on a philosophical career, it would be right for everybody, and a man cannot decide whether it is right for himself or not without considering his own psychology. It may be objected that this makes the principle of universality of no importance, since the circumstances will never be exactly the same for two different agents, if only because the agents are different men, and indeed even for the same agent on two different occasions. But only a small proportion of the circumstances will be ethically relevant, and these might well be similar. Of all the multitudinous circumstances of past history and psychological make-up which differentiate me from another man, only a relatively few will be relevant to the question whether either of us should take up philosophy and probably none at all to the obligation to pay our ordinary debts. One might just as well argue that the "uniformity of nature," or the principle that the same event may be expected under the same conditions, has no relevance to physical science because the conditions are never quite the same on two different occasions. The main point is that I am never entitled to advance on behalf of my own action an excuse which I should not be prepared to accept from anybody else. If I am to maintain that some act is obligatory for A and not for B, I must be able to point to some difference between the circumstances or dispositions of A and B which will account for the difference in obligation, just as the point of the uniformity of nature for the scientist lies in the rule that, if different things happen, the difference must be explained by a difference in the conditions.

Kant, however, held not merely that the same act was always right or wrong for everybody under the same conditions, physical and psychological, but that there are a number of classes of acts which are always wrong under all conditions. Thus he maintained that it was never right to tell lies even in order to save human life from a murderer. This conclusion is very difficult to accept, but if we do not accept it we must admit that Ethics is not *a priori* in the way in which Kant held it was, since we may then occasionally set a general rule aside on account of empirical consequences.

This point has sometimes been expressed by saying that Kant's ethics ignores consequences. This is unfair, and if true would make his ethics a complete absurdity not worth serious study. The truth is that Kant allows us to take account of consequences in order to apply an ethical law but not in order to establish the validity of the law or to make an exception to the law. In order to apply the law that we must not lie we are obviously bound to take account of consequences up to a point. We must take account of the likely effects of our words on the person to whom they are addressed if we are to be understood. But we must not, Kant thinks, justify the general law against lying by arguing that lying usually does more evil than good. This he would say was true, but did not constitute the reason why lying was wrong. Still less, Kant insists, must we argue that we are entitled to lie in a particular case because in this case lying will do more good than evil. It is in this sense that Kant objected to taking account of consequences in deciding what we ought to do. We may note that the law that we ought to help others still more obviously requires a consideration of consequences for its application, but Kant still seems to say that the ultimate justification of it is to be found not in its good consequences but in the fact that we should be in some way acting inconsistently if we broke it, i.e. making an arbitrary exception in our own favour to a rule which we cannot help wishing should be generally observed.

Further, we should note a sense in which Kant is quite obviously right in saying that consequences do not matter, namely, when he insists that the morality of an action and the worth of the agent are not affected by the actual as opposed to the intended or at least foreseeable consequences. In many novels the most dastardly act of the villain turns out to be just the unintended means of bringing about the triumph of the hero and his marriage to the heroine, but if this really happened the beneficial effects of the villain's action could not in the least be accounted to his credit since he intended the reverse, nor could a well-intentioned man be blamed for any unforeseeable consequences of his acts, however deplorable.

But very few writers on ethics since Kant have been prepared to attach so little importance to consequences as he did in deciding how we ought to act. Kant conceived ethics as a set of *a priori* laws which each possessed strict universality, but this view is hard to maintain. The question is of great practical importance especially, though not only, in connection with war. In all wars some, and in the last war almost all, generally accepted ethical rules of action were violated, and their violation was justified as a necessary means to averting still greater evils. So it seems that anybody who refuses to admit that consequences can ever justify the breach of a general ethical law ought to be a conscientious objector to military service.[1] But, even apart from war, there are liable to be cases where one of the alleged universal laws conflicts with another, and then whichever decision is right the laws cannot both be universal. Thus the law not to tell

---

[1] Kant, however, did not take this view, I think inconsistently.

lies and the law to save life conflict if I am asked by a murderer about the whereabouts of his intended victim, or by an invalid on the verge of heart failure for news of a son who I know has died when he still thinks him alive and well. When this happens we must admit an exception to at least one of the laws, for since I must either lie or not, it must be right either to lie or to sacrifice a life which I could have saved. We cannot escape the difficulty by saying we ought to keep silent, because there are circumstances in which refusal to answer a question would be equivalent to letting the questioner know the truth. Kant apparently intended to meet such situations by always giving preference to the negative over the positive law, but this seems arbitrary. And in cases where two laws conflict it is hard to see how we can rationally decide between them except by considering the goodness or badness of the consequences. However important it is to tell the truth and however evil to lie, there are surely cases where much greater evils still can only be averted by a lie, and is lying wrong then? Would it not be justifiable for a diplomat to lie, and indeed break most general moral laws, if it were practically certain that this and this alone would avert a third world-war? Some people would answer—No, but they could only defend their position not by argument but by appeal to self-evidence—which Kant does not make—and while it may be self-evident that lying is always evil, it is surely not self-evident that it is always wrong. To incur a lesser evil in order to avert a much greater might well be right, and if that is the case as regards a lie, the lie is evil but not wrong. Without committing myself to the view that absolute pacifism is right, I must however add that I feel considerable sympathy with those who say that it must be wrong to pursue even a good end by evil means because the bad means will taint and poison the results they produce, and because once we adopt this line we are on a slippery slope and do not know where to stop. (Almost all the great political crimes of history have been justified by their perpetrators as means to the greatest good, but of course the fact that a line of justification is often grossly abused does not prove that it is never to be adopted at all, though as I have suggested it is exceedingly difficult to draw the line.) But I do not see how this argument can possibly be carried so far as to exclude all deceit or injustice even, e.g., to save life, and it is at any rate one which appeals to consequences, so as against Kant it must be admitted that it is hard to avoid giving the latter a decisive rôle where two laws conflict.

Kant introduces two other supreme principles besides the one which tells us to act as if the principle of our action were to be law universal. He indeed for obscure reasons (with which the general reader need not bother) claims that the three are only different formulations of the same truth, but I do not think this can be defended. In any case they are to all appearance different. The second principle reads, "Act so as to treat humanity both in your own person and in that of every other man always as an end and never only as a means." (Note the word "only": we treat a man as a means whenever we allow him to do us a service, and that of course is not wrong, provided we treat him also as an end-in-himself.) Now these words of Kant have had as much influence as perhaps any sentence written by a philosopher; they serve indeed as a slogan of the whole liberal and democratic movement of recent times. They rule out slavery, exploitation, lack of respect for another's dignity and personality, the making of the individual a mere tool of the State, violations of rights. They formulate the greatest moral idea of the day, perhaps one might add the greatest moral (as distinct from "religious") idea of Christianity. But without casting any aspersions on their value, we must point out that they can only serve as a guide to tell us which particular actions to perform if we have some positive idea of the ends of man, so the second principle like the first seems to need supplementation by reference to the positive goods which are to be brought about by its adoption.

The third principle is defined as "the idea of the will of

every rational being as a universally legislating will," but this, beyond saying that we are bound by the laws of morality because we realize that we are so bound, adds little to the first law and does not itself give further help in determining what we ought to do in particular cases.

The main upshot of the argument of this chapter is to suggest that Kant's ethics, in so far as it is regarded as a means to determining what is right, needs at any rate to be supplemented and possibly altogether replaced by a point of view which will be more ultilitarian, not in the sense of admitting that happiness is the only good, but in the sense of deriving the rightness or wrongness of acts from the good or harm they do. We might disagree with the hedonistic utilitarian as to what is good and yet agree with him in holding that the only thing which makes an act right or wrong is the good or evil it produces or is liable to produce. We have seen how Kant's principles require utilitarian supplementation, the first in order to enable us to decide which ethical precept to obey when there is a conflict between two, the second in order to provide that concrete idea of end without which the principle of treating humanity as an end-in-itself cannot be practically applied. Kant may possibly have been right in holding that the essence of morality and the supreme good for man lies in the nature of the will and yet mistaken in holding that the criterion needed to tell us which acts are right and which wrong is to be found in anything but the consequences which can reasonably be anticipated from action. The strength of such a position was not apparent to Kant because he kept thinking of some form of hedonism as the only alternative to his view, and ignored the possibility of a theory which, without taking the hedonist view of good and evil, still derived the obligatoriness or wrongness of an action from its good or bad effects. It remains to consider, in the next chapter, whether this type of utilitarianism is itself capable of defence. In the meantime we must note with gratitude Kant's description of the specifically moral element in our nature, which may be able to stand in the main independently of his theory of the criteria for determining what is right, as it does stand independently of the general philosophy which he connects with it.

Chapter 5

The Pursuit of the Good

THE DEVELOPMENT of the argument now suggests a theory according to which the criterion of the rightness or wrongness of acts[1] is to be found solely in the good or evil they are liable to produce but the good is not identified with happiness or the evil with pain. To this view has been given the name of *Ideal Utilitarianism* in opposition to *Hedonistic Utilitarianism,* which both makes productiveness of good or evil the criterion and also identifies good with pleasure and evil with pain. Leading exponents of the former view have been H. Rashdall[2] (1858–1924) and G. E. Moore[3] (1873–   ). It is certainly the most plausible view of the ultimate criterion that we have yet considered. It has the advantage over Kant of emphasizing consequences and over ordinary utilitarianism of recognizing other goods besides pleasure, among which goods we may include that of moral character on which Kant insisted, and also the goods of human love and intellectual and aesthetic experience which he left not specifically recognized and seems to have indeed regarded (at least at the time when he wrote his main ethical works) as valuable only as a means to pleasure. All these may be regarded as good-in-themselves by the ideal utilitarian. At the same time the principle that the rightness[4] of an action

[1] Though not of their praiseworthiness or blameworthiness. These characteristics will be discussed in Chap. 8.
[2] *Theory of Good and Evil* (vol. I, chap. VII).
[3] *Principia Ethica* (1903) and *Ethics* (1912).
[4] For relation between *right* and *ought* and distinction between *right* and *the right, v.* above p. 15.

is determined by its liability to produce good is retained. And indeed what better or what other ultimate reason could there be, one may ask, for doing anything than that it brings into existence good or lessens or prevents evil? Surely the object of life is to leave the world better than we found it, and as much better as we can? Does this not provide the only possible rational basis for ethics? And with admittedly right acts we can normally easily point to the good they do and in the case of wrong acts to the evil.

According to the view we are now discussing the ultimate way of deciding what action is the right one in a given situation is to estimate how much good each alternative action of which we can think will produce, balance against this the evil, and decide in favour of the action which shows the greatest balance of good over evil. I say the "ultimate" way because it is quite consistent and reasonable for a person who holds this view to admit that in practice we can often use general rules without appealing directly to the consequences in each particular case. Provided the general rules themselves are justified by their utility in producing good in most cases, it is usually safer, he will say, to rely on them than to work out each case for oneself by a direct calculation of consequences. He need not hold that a good man will never refrain from telling any lie which occurs to him till he has first worked out the consequences of telling it. In most cases at least, it is obviously sufficient to rely on the generalization that lies usually produce bad consequences, which generalization is certainly justified empirically. There will still be plenty of room for the direct calculation of consequences where there is no general rule applicable or where two rules conflict. We have seen that such conflicts arise, and it must be admitted that it is difficult to see how we can settle them except by an appeal to consequences or to see how anything about the consequences can be relevant to what we ought or ought not to do except their goodness or badness.

However there now arise two serious complications.[5]

[5] These also apply to hedonistic utilitarianism.

In the first place, our forecasts of consequences can only be probable not certain, hence we have to take into consideration not merely the amount of anticipated good or evil but also the degree of probability with which we can reasonably anticipate it. It may be much better to have £1000 than £100, but still a wise man will not pay £100 for a very slight chance of winning £1000. And there are many cases where an action leads to very unfortunate consequences but the agent is not blameworthy because he had no good reason for anticipating as at all probable these consequences. I could not be blamed for having asked a man in a normal physical state to come and see me because he slipped and broke his leg on the way. Are we then to say that the action we ought to do is the absolutely most desirable one, i.e. on the utilitarian view the one which will in fact produce the best consequences, or simply the action which it is best to choose at the time in view of its probable consequences? To ask the man at that time may well have been an action which I ought to perform in the latter sense but not in the former. In my statement of the theory at the beginning of this chapter I intended to cover both alternatives by the use of the vague word "liable." The answer is that we may say either, provided we recognize that the word has these two different senses and we are clear and make it clear to our hearers which we are using, but in fact "ought" is very rarely used in the former sense except by philosophers.[6] In any case it is important to be clear that we cannot *blame* a man because he does not do what he ought in the former sense of "ought," but only because he does not do it in the latter. Disastrous consequences which could not possibly be foreseen are only a ground for pronouncing an act to be unfortunate, never for pronouncing it blameworthy. Indeed, even if a man does not do what he ought in the latter sense, i.e. choose most wisely, he cannot be blamed morally if he has made an honest mistake as to a matter of fact, but he can be blamed intellectually, i.e. pronounced relatively unwise.

---

[6] e.g. G. E. Moore, *Ethics,* pp. 118-121.

But the concept of blame will be discussed later. Here it is sufficient just to distinguish the two questions: (a) Is a particular act right? (b) Supposing the agent to have done wrong—was he morally to blame for doing so? It is the former kind of question we are discussing here, not the latter. We can cast doubt on the rightness of a man's policy without impugning his good faith or good will. But we cannot exercise our good will unless we at least try to find out what action is really right, and this is the question to which ideal utilitarians seek to provide the answer. If by "right" is meant the action objectively most desirable, their answer will be in terms of the good and evil actually produced; if "wisest to choose," in terms of the good and evil which can be reasonably anticipated by the agent in view of the data at his disposal.

Secondly, it may be objected to ideal utilitarianism that its criterion is quite inapplicable because we cannot possibly foresee all the consequences of any action. For the consequences of an action in the next five minutes will produce other consequences in the following five, and so on for ever or to the end of time. Here I think the distinction between the two senses of "ought" is very helpful. If by the right action or the action I ought to do is meant the absolutely most desirable action, I do not see how in view of the limitations in our power of forecasting consequences we can determine what that is, but if what is meant is the action that it is wisest to choose this need not be beyond our capacity. We cannot anticipate at all the remoter consequences of any of our actions, but if we cannot do so they cannot figure in deciding what is the wisest action for us to choose, though they would in deciding what is absolutely the most desirable. If we do not know what they are likely to be at all and have no reason to think they will be good rather than bad or vice versa, the only wise course is to ignore them. Or at least the existence of unknown consequences may either be ignored or serve as just an additional reason in favour of doing what has good effects as far as we can see and eschewing what has evil. For it may be argued that, in so far as the act and its earlier foreseeable consequences are good, the presumption is that its later unforeseeable consequences will probably be more good than evil. Good will surely tend on the whole to produce good, and evil to produce evil.

On an utilitarian view, whether we are to judge an act right or wrong will depend partly on our judgement as to its factual consequences and partly on our estimate of the value or reverse of these consequences. We might be tempted to think that the way to reach a decision is to analyse the likely consequences into their component elements, estimate the value of each of these, and then sum their values so as to determine the value of the whole, but this may be questioned. For, firstly, the mathematical analogy may be attacked. Secondly, it may well happen that two things which are good in themselves are not good in combination or are more or less good than one would expect from considering them separately. The enjoyment of a joke is good and the appreciation of the tragic climax of a great drama is good, but the combination of the two experiences at the same time would be much less good because aesthetically inappropriate. Pleasure is good and it is good to know the truth, but the knowledge that another man is suffering pain combined with a feeling of pleasure at that man's pain is not good but evil. On the other hand a good poem or picture (or rather the experience of it) has a value as a whole much greater than we should expect if we merely considered successively in isolation from each other the separate lines or figures, still more, words or microscopic colour patches, or the perceptions of these. The point is that the value of something depends not merely on its component elements but also on their interrelations, and in that case we cannot count on obtaining an adequate idea of its value by merely summing the elements without taking account of their interrelations. We do not necessarily improve a situation by adding indiscriminately things which are good in themselves, but only by adding them in the right times and places.

So the way to evaluate the consequences of an action does not lie through any quasi-mathematical calculus; all we can do is consider all the appreciable advantages and disadvantages of which we can think in regard to each of the alternative actions between which we choose, and having done this see what the total impression is on our mind, taking into account also the degree of probability of attaining the results we desire and the risk of any unintended evils. It sounds very complicated, yet we obviously have on any view to do something of this sort when we make ethical decisions which cannot be settled merely by appealing to an obvious rule. For we have at least constantly to take consequences into account, even if the utilitarian is not right in saying that, for deciding what we ought to do, the good and evil consequences *alone* matter. There are no general rules by which we can settle without considering consequences whether to accept a given post, how to spend our surplus income, how best to educate people. However it is not that we have to go through an elaborate reasoning process of formal logic in which all these factors serve as premises—such an account is certainly far too complicated to do justice to the actual ethical reasoning even of philosophers—but that, having thought as far as possible of all importantly relevant considerations, we then see in what state of mind we are put by our whole process of thinking, i.e. how we are impressed by the influence all these considerations taken together. The chief way in which we make ethical mistakes as regards particular actions is through failing to attend, or to attend sufficiently, to some of the effects, especially relatively remote though clearly foreseeable ones or ones which appeal less than others to our tastes and desires.

What is the good which we are to aim at producing? This question is misleading because it suggests that there is ultimately only one kind of thing which is intrinsically good, that all the various goods can be brought under a single head, and we must not assume that this is necessarily so. It may be that there are a number of different kinds of good which have nothing in common except their goodness. The only very widely accepted and very thorough-going attempt to reduce all the different goods to a single one is hedonism which finds the good exclusively in pleasure, and this view we have rejected as inadequate. One limitation indeed almost all moral philosophers impose on what is good, they agree in insisting that it must relate to conscious beings, but this still leaves scope for a great variety of different goods. The mind has commonly been classified as having three aspects, that of feeling, that of knowledge and that of will and action, and happiness or pleasure has been regarded as the specific good of feeling, truth or rather its attainment of knowledge, and moral virtue of will and action. It is not clear how we are able to include in this classification aesthetic value (beauty), love and religious values. But perhaps we may say that these are values relating to all three sides of our nature at once, not to any one by itself.

From our earlier discussion of hedonistic utilitarianism there emerged the conclusion that we must regard one way of distribution as inherently "fairer" and therefore better than another. This may be made an objection to ideal utilitarianism on the ground that a fairer distribution is better than one less fair even if the same amount of good be distributed, so that the quantity of good produced or evil averted is not the sole criterion of rightness. However the ideal utilitarian may, unlike the hedonistic utilitarian, reply by including fairness of distribution itself under the intrinsic goods to be recognized. In that case we should have to add to the good distributed the good of distributing it fairly and set against it the evil of distributing it unfairly. This would be another illustration of the principle just mentioned that the value of a whole depends not only on the values of its parts but also on their relations.

If we are to say there is only one good, the most promising candidate seems to me to be harmony. When we are in harmony on the feeling side with ourselves and our environment we have happiness; when we are in harmony on the intellectual side with reality, we have truth and wisdom; when in harmony with other men, social virtue and love; when in harmony with God, religious peace. And aesthetic experience is very commonly also regarded as the enjoyment of a kind of harmony. But the claims of harmony to be the sole good are hard to reconcile with the fact that one of the things we must account as most eminently good is a heroic struggle against difficulties and with the fact that a worse man is often more in harmony with himself and with society than a better. All this suggests that it is at least doubtful whether we can produce any tidy list of things good-in-themselves. Even if the different goods belong to the same genus, they are different species and have to be considered separately.

It may be asked how we can possibly balance against each other such different kinds of good. They seem to have no common measure. But in any case on any view we must balance against each other goods of very different kinds if we are to come to a decision about acts which further some at the expense of others. This must apply to any theory which has any reference to consequences and not only to ideal utilitarianism, and even if we do not agree that rightness depends wholly on consequences, we can hardly eliminate the reference to consequences altogether. We cannot of course determine that one set of good consequences following from an act are, e.g. 2.47 times as good as another set, but we may be able roughly to balance the one against the other. Having surveyed two sets of good or evil consequences we can see that the advantage lies with one side and decide accordingly.

Some of the objections brought against hedonistic utilitarianism are also brought against the view we are now discussing, but it is easier for the ideal utilitarian to answer them because he can introduce other values besides pleasure and appeal to the bad effect of certain acts on character as an end-in-itself. Thus he can say that lying, even where it gives more pleasure than pain, is bad for the character of the person who lies, and that this grave evil may often outweigh the gain in pleasure even where, if we only considered the latter, we might think it right to lie. He need not and will not say that lying is *never* right, but then can we really say this? Might not a lie well be justified to save an invalid from death or prevent a war? And he will need to admit the rightness of lying less frequently than would a consistent hedonistic utilitarian.

Nevertheless it is still often felt that ideal utilitarianism is not ethically satisfactory. One reason for this is because it seems to lead to the principle that "the end justifies the means," a principle commonly rejected as immoral. If the end is the greatest good possible and the means necessary to attain it include great moral evils such as deceit, injustice, gross violation of individual rights or even murder, the utilitarian will have to say that these things are morally justified, provided only their moral evil is exceeded by the goodness of the results, and this seems a downright immoral doctrine, and certainly a very dangerous one (as is shown by its applications in recent times in politics). It is not however by any means clear that the people who thus misapplied it were really doing what was conducive to the greatest good, even if they thought they were. It may be clear to a Communist but it is certainly very far from being clear to me that the furtherance of Communism is a good, still less that it is so great a good as to justify the evil means used to spread it, nor is it clear that these evil means really make it more or less likely to spread and maintain itself in the long run. As we saw with the Nazis, evil means have a way of serving their purpose for a time but then recoiling like a boomerang on the people who employ them. And in general it is very hard to be sure that the evil means which seem to be needed do really serve the end for which they are adopted or do so without producing evil consequences that outweigh their benefits. One may argue here from the very uncertainty of our predictions. Only a fraction of the total consequences can be predicted by us, and there is much reason to think that the adoption of evil means is liable to produce evil beyond what we can predict. There is good empirical evidence for this, even if we are not prepared to back it by the plausible *a priori* argument that evil produces evil, not good. Lies do tend to get found out and "dirty tricks" to recoil on their authors in all sorts of unexpected ways. This argument is particularly important in politics where the effects of actions are particularly uncertain. Any reader could no doubt mention quite a number of politicians in the world who in his opinion would be better dead than alive, but political assassinations have rarely led to the results their perpetrators anticipated or desired. If it is really clear that the evil means are needed to lead to results which outweigh their badness, the ideal utilitarian must sanction them, but this will not be nearly so common as it may at first sight seem, and certainly nobody but a thorough-going pacifist can throw a stone at him for doing so. Most people, and not only Communists and Nazis, have been prepared, rightly or wrongly, to sanction the appallingly evil means involved in modern war where the alternative evils were conceived as sufficiently great.

Yet it is very much of a paradox to say that a man is no more under a special obligation to one to whom he has made a promise or to his own parents, children, or wife than to a total stranger, the sole obligation being to produce as much good for *anyone* as possible. Again it is a paradox to say that, if a man has done avoidable harm, he is under no more obligation to repair it than is anybody else not at all concerned in the damage. And it is a further paradox to say that it is as much a violation of obligation for me knowingly to do something which involves unnecessary pain for myself as it is for me to do something which involves equal pain for another person, even though the amount of evil is equal. The utilitarian may reply by justifying the obligations in question indirectly. He may say that for various fairly obvious reasons it is conducive to the general good that people should be under special obligations to their close relatives and to those to whom they have made promises. He may say that it is socially useful that people should be under some obligation to make good the damage they carelessly or deliberately inflict, because they are then less likely to inflict it. And he may say that, since men are liable to be more averse to or more quick to realize the danger of pain for themselves than for others, they do not need to dwell on their obligation not to hurt themselves unnecessarily but do need to dwell on their obligation not to hurt others. But such an account does not correspond to our ordinary ethical thinking, since it makes the obligations in question not direct but indirect. On such a view a man has no more obligation to his wife or children as such in themselves than he has to any stranger, it is merely that he can do more good on the whole by making special efforts to minister to their wants than by devoting equal attention to ministering to the wants of strangers. His obligations to his family are only derivative from his indiscriminate obligations to everybody. Yet it would seem ungracious for a man to say to good parents or any benefactors by whom he has been immensely helped at great cost to themselves —I am under no special obligation to you more than to anybody else, but my obligation to people in general requires me to make special efforts to do what is to your benefit.

> The essential defect of the "ideal utilitarian" theory is that it ignores, or at least does not do full justice to, the highly personal character of duty. If the only duty is to produce the maximum of good, the question who is to have the good—whether it is myself, or my benefactor, or a person to whom I have made a promise to confer that good on him, or a mere fellow man to whom I stand in no such special relation—should make no difference to my having a duty to produce that good. But we are all in fact sure that it makes a vast difference.[7]

It is felt that people should not be regarded in Ethics merely as receptacles into which to pour as much good as possible but as being in special individual relations to the agent.

These considerations together with some logical difficulties about the derivation of obligation from good led to a revolt against Ideal Utilitarianism which has found its most developed and coherent expression in the work of an

---

[7] Ross, *The Right and the Good,* p. 22.

Oxford philosopher, Sir David Ross (1877–   ).[8] His is essentially a compromise theory, but it is not necessarily any the worse for that. It seems highly likely that the truest theory available in Ethics will be one which does not rely on a single simple principle at the risk of one-sidedness but somehow combines the strong points of various different views. Thus the new theory seeks to modify the exclusive utilitarian insistence on consequences, but still gives the latter a leading place among the criteria for determining whether an action is right, and it defends *a priori* laws in ethics not derived from the good produced without maintaining that they hold in all circumstances, as did Kant. In order to expound the theory we must first explain a new technical term, *prima facie duty*. This phrase is used in a special sense in the writings of Ross to signify an obligation that only holds subject to not being overridden by a superior obligation. It does not mean, as the words might suggest, an only apparent obligation, but a real, though not an absolute, one. Thus we are said to have a "*prima facie duty*" to keep promises because, while the fact that we have made a promise is always in itself a strong moral reason for keeping it, this reason may in exceptional circumstances be outweighed by a still more pressing obligation, e.g. to save life. Ross mentions the following *prima facie* duties.[9]

(1) The obligation to keep promises. A sub-case of this is the obligation not to tell lies since we by a tacit understanding commit ourselves to tell the truth when we use language in contexts in which we are supposed to be imparting information. (2) The obligation to make restitution for harm done. (3) The obligation of "gratitude" to return benefits. Under this heading falls the obligation to our parents. He does not say under what heading he would

---

[8] *The Right and the Good* (1930); *Foundations of Ethics* (1939).
[9] *The Right and the Good,* p. 21. He gives their number as six not seven, because he lists what I have called 1 and 2 as 1a and 1b, but I have found it more convenient for exposition to use in all cases separate numerical heads.

put the obligation of a parent to his children. (4) The obligation to distribute rewards and punishments in accordance with merit. (5) The obligation to do good to others. (6) The obligation to improve ourselves in respect of virtue and intelligence. (7) The obligation to abstain from injuring others. The last three can obviously be brought under utilitarianism, except that Ross insisted against the utilitarians that we are under no obligation to further *our own* happiness, and that the obligation to abstain from harming others is more stringent than the obligation to do them good so that we are not entitled to harm A in order to do B a good which just and only just balances the harm to A. Ross thinks that the fourth obligation also may be justified simply by a reference to the good produced, since a state of affairs in which rewards and punishments are distributed justly is better than one in which they are not. But the first three he thinks not derivable in any utilitarian way. It does not seem any better that a richer man to whom I owe £100 or on whom I have inflicted £100 damage should have the money than that I should, as we should certainly feel if he picked it up in the street, yet I have a *prima facie* duty to pay it. Hence it is not, according to him, the consequences but the mere fact that I have made a promise which puts me under an obligation to keep it, as long as the person to whom I have made the promise does not release me. And similarly he holds that it may be my duty to confer a lesser benefit on those who have benefited me or whom I have injured rather than a greater on those who have not stood in such relations to me.

When I am under a *prima facie* obligation to do so-and-so and this does not conflict with another of the *prima facie* obligations, including those dependent on the production of good and avoidance of evil consequences, I always ought to do it. But it often happens that two *prima facie* obligations conflict, and in these cases Ross maintains that no general rules for deciding between them can be given. We just have to judge each case on its individual merits, and our decision may be liable to great uncertainty.

But we must do the best we can, and decisions, though not certain or derivable by strict inference, may still be more or less reasonable. Thus he admits that we are not under an absolute obligation to keep a promise if the consequences of doing so are sufficiently disastrous, but he is unable, any more than any other philosopher, to supply rules for determining exactly how bad they have to be in order to counteract the *prima facie* obligation to keep it. And similarly with all *prima facie* duties, except that many of these are presumably somewhat less stringent and less definite than that of promise-keeping and would therefore require a lesser degree of evil to justify their violation. So he distinguishes sharply *prima facie* from absolute duties. The latter depend on the former in that we cannot have an absolute duty to do anything unless we first have a *prima facie* duty to do it, but the converse is not true since *prima facie* duties often conflict with each other. Great concessions are made to utilitarianism in that many of the *prima facie* duties are directly derived from the good their fulfilment produces, or the evil it avoids, and even those which are made independent of this good and harm may be overruled in favour of the others in cases where the consequences of carrying them out are sufficiently undesirable. But the utilitarian proposition that we ought always to do what produces the greatest good is denied: the amount of good and evil produced is only one consideration, and it should sometimes be overruled in favour of others.

Prior to the formulation of Ross's theory the utilitarian was in the favourable position of being faced with no alternative theory which was at once clear and plausible. The only clear alternatives to some form of utilitarianism seemed to be: (1) an extreme intuitionism according to which we just saw what was right in each particular case without any reference to consequences or general rules of action, (2) a view according to which we knew a number of ethical laws to hold absolutely universally without regard to consequences. Most philosophers will certainly find ideal utilitarianism preferable to either of these two views, but it is not so clear that it is preferable to the subtler theory of Ross.

Even if the latter theory turn out not to be finally acceptable on its philosophic merits, it must be admitted that it is highly important in the following respect. It does constitute the nearest approach yet made to an account of how we actually think about ethical questions at the common-sense level. Whatever our philosophical conclusions, it is very desirable to have a clear account of this, and it is certain that at the common-sense level we are not strict utilitarians but think in terms of a number of obligations not all derived by us from utility, even if this in fact constitutes their final justification. But it is widely felt that the theory gives less in the way of an explanation or justification of our duties than a philosopher requires and than is provided by utilitarianism. It seems unsatisfactory to most philosophers to admit as a final account of ethics a theory which just leaves us with a heap of unconnected and underived *prima facie* duties, to be accepted as self-evidently obligatory without any reason that can be adduced for saying these acts are our duties. Against this the utilitarian does provide for all our duties a rational ground which explains why they are duties. The difference between the two views must not indeed be exaggerated here. As Ross, if questioned why promise-keeping is a *prima facie* duty, can only say that this is self-evident, so the utilitarian, if asked why one kind of thing is good-in-itself and another bad or how he knows this, has to fall back also on self-evidence. Again, just as Ross has to balance different *prima facie* duties against each other in cases of conflict without any logical as opposed to intuitive means of deciding between them, so the utilitarian has to balance different goods. Yet it somehow looks more like an ultimate self-evident truth that some things are good-in-themselves than that we ought to perform certain acts. The latter statement seems to call for the question—Why? while the former does not do so. We do not need to ask why happiness and virtue are good, we just see them to be so. It also seems evident to me and to most philosophers (including Ross himself) that to say that some act produces good effects is to give a reason for doing it, and that therefore the utilitarian theory does provide an adequate reason for doing some things and not doing others. Further, it is very hard to believe that it can ever be our duty deliberately to produce less good than we might, as it would have to be on Ross's view on many occasions, i.e. whenever one of the *prima facie* duties not based on utilitarian considerations outweighs those which are based on them.

And the ideal utilitarian can have at his disposal ways of replying to Ross's arguments which the hedonistic utilitarian has not. For, where his opponent says we have a *prima facie* duty to do so-and-so, e.g. keep promises, he can always reply that it is intrinsically good to do so, or at least that the act of refusing to perform the *prima facie* duty is intrinsically bad. This would indeed imply a considerable transformation in his view as most usually understood, for it involves the admission that the rightness or wrongness of acts is not always dependent on consequences over and above the acts. But it would be by no means incompatible with the fundamental utilitarian principle that rightness depends on the balance of good over evil produced. For if anything is good-in-itself other than pleasure, or bad-in-itself other than pain, it is only reasonable to suppose that certain morally significant acts are, and if this is so we must before we can determine whether an act is right on utilitarian principles consider its own value or disvalue as well as that of its consequences. Ideal utilitarians have not expressed themselves too clearly on this point, but I do not know of any who rule the possibility out. Indeed it is excessively difficult to see how they could both maintain that virtue is good-in-itself (as they would almost always do) and deny that virtuous acts are good in this way. For virtue can only be realized in virtuous acts and is apart from them a mere vacuous potentiality, of value only hypothetically and not in actual fact. So there is nothing inconsistent in an ideal utilitarian ascribing intrinsic goodness and badness to acts. If this line is taken utilitarianism is very hard to refute, but it may be asked whether there is really any very important difference between saying it is intrinsically bad to break promises and saying that we have a *prima facie* duty not to break them. This point is strengthened if we adopt the plausible view that "good" in this context is to be defined as what ought to be chosen or furthered. For in that case to say that something is intrinsically good is just to say that it ought to be chosen or furthered for its own sake, and to say that it is intrinsically bad is to say that of itself it ought to be avoided. And this is again the same as to say that we have a *prima facie* duty respectively to choose or avoid it. On the other hand I do feel in any case that the test of *prima facie* duties should lie partly in their coherence in a rational system of ethics and not just in their self-evidence as separate principles of action.

The contending views now seem to have been brought very close together. Even if the definition I have suggested of "good" is wrong, does it really much matter whether we use the term "intrinsically good" or the term "*prima facie* duty?" It is hard to think that it does. Yet connected with the controversy there are two issues which do seem to me of great importance in Ethics. (*a*) While there is little difference between the defender of *prima facie* duties and a utilitarian who admits that, e.g. the keeping of promises is intrinsically good or the breaking of them intrinsically bad, there is a good deal of difference between him and the kind of utilitarian who tries to derive the rightness or wrongness of acts simply from consequences beyond the acts. The difference may even be of great practical importance, since the two may well take quite different views as to the legitimacy of using evil means for good ends. Other things being equal, the latter type of thinker will obviously be more inclined to think them legitimate than the former. (*b*) There is a very important difference between what is often called the Greek view of ethics which thinks of the right life as consisting primarily in the pursuit of valuable concrete ends and what is often called the Hebrew view which thinks of it as consisting primarily in obedience to the moral law. My own sympathy is rather with the former, whether or not "good" can be formally analysed in terms of "ought," since at any rate most laws seem to depend for their bindingness on the ends they further, but there is no doubt a place in ethics for both concepts. We can certainly no more dispense with

78 / Ethics

the notion of obligation than with that of good even if the former be subordinate to the latter.

Chapter 6

Attempts to Define "Good" and "Ought"[1]

WE HAVE SO FAR considered what kinds of things are good and how we are to decide what is our duty, but not what the words good and ought (or duty) mean. Yet the latter question has also been very much debated by moral philosophers. Clearly we could not discuss ethical questions at all or make the ethical judgements we all make in ordinary life if we had not some idea of the meaning of terms such as good, bad, duty, etc., but it is very clear on the other hand that we do not prior to study understand the terms with the precision required by a philosopher, and a great deal of effort has accordingly been exercised to find definitions for them. That the question of definition is not merely a verbal one but is of great importance for our whole outlook on Ethics will soon be clear from what follows.

The problem of definition is complicated by the fact that the terms we seek to define are liable to be used in several different senses, and this is particularly the case with the chief ethical terms, *good and ought,* but I cannot possibly go into all the complications involved. However I pointed out in the first chapter[2] a fundamental sense of "good," the sense in which the word stands for what is intrinsically good or good as an end in itself as distinguished in particular from what is good only as a means,

---

[1] I am indebted to the Macmillan Company of New York and Messrs. Routledge and Kegan Paul for permission to use my book *The Definition of Good* in compiling this chapter and Chapter 7.

[2] *v.* above p. 12 ff.

i.e. as an instrument for producing other things which are good in the more fundamental sense of the term. It is round this sense that the controversy has centred. Now in a very important book, *Principia Ethica* (1903), the Cambridge philosopher, G. E. Moore, maintained that the correct answer to the question is that good in this sense has no definition. This will seem at first sight a very unsatisfactory answer, but when we realize just what he means by "definition," I think we shall see that some terms must be indefinable if anything is to be defined at all. For he uses "definable" as equivalent to "analysable," and it is clear, as I have already pointed out,[3] that we cannot go on analysing *ad infinitum*. If we ask what something, A, is and are then told that it is BCD, this will not help us unless we know what B, C, and D are. If we are then told that B consists of FGH, C of I, etc., the same question will arise once again. We cannot understand a definition of anything unless we understand certain terms, themselves not defined, of which the definition is composed. But how can we do this? We cannot understand them by knowing their definition, because they have none, so the only answer is—by direct experience. We have experience of certain characteristics and thus know what they are like, as we could not do without having exeprienced them. To take an example, we are acquainted with various colours directly by experience, and this is how we know what is meant by, e.g. "red." We cannot propound any definition of a colour that will enable a colour-blind man to know what it is like, but those who are not colour-blind certainly do know. The absence of a definition is in no way an obstacle to the possession of such knowledge. Similarly it may be contended that we know sufficiently what good is by the experience of apprehending good things. Goodness is of course a very different kind of characteristic from a colour, but they might still well resemble each other in being immediately apprehended and in being indefinable. We see some things (at least experiences) directly to be good, and to do this involves at the same time seeing what

---

[3] *v.* above p. 19.

goodness is like, as to see a red rose is also to see what redness is like. This would not prevent good being definable in some other sense. If, e.g., we could discover some characteristic which always accompanied goodness and never occurred unless goodness were present, we might define good in terms of that characteristic, as the physicist defines a colour in terms of the light-waves which accompany or cause its perception. But such a definition would not tell us what the quality good is like any more than the physicist's definitions of colours in terms of wave-lengths will tell a colour-blind man what the colours are like.

The distinction between the two senses of "definition" may be brought out by this illustration. Suppose a future physiologist to discover a modification of the brain which accompanied every good experience and action and never occurred without being accompanied by a good experience or action, and suppose (which seems plausible) that the only intrinsically good things are experiences and actions or analysable in terms of experiences and actions. The brain-modifications would then be co-present with goodness whenever it occurred, but it would not follow in the least that "good" just *meant* "accompanied by this brain-modification" or that good was *identical* with property of being accompanied by it. It would assuredly not provide a definition in Moore's sense of the term. Now it is Moore's sense of definition which will give the essential nature of what is to be defined as opposed to its accompaniments. To maintain that good is indefinable is not to maintain that we cannot know what it is like or that we cannot say anything about it but only that it is not reducible to anything else. Some properties are complex, and these can be defined in terms of the elements which make them up, but Moore insists that good is simple and therefore cannot be thus defined.

It has been asked why we desire to produce what has this indefinable quality of goodness, but the answer surely would be that this is how we are made. We can never give a logical explanation why we have the desires we have. What follows necessarily from the goodness of something is not that we desire it in fact, but that other things being equal, we ought to produce it, if possible. In fact we are not so constituted that we are unattracted by the desire to produce good; if we were never attracted by it, we could not produce it except by accident, since we cannot act without any desire,[4] and we should consequently be under no obligation to do so. A person who regards good as a simple quality has not to explain why he desires it any more than we have to or can explain logically why we desire food that tastes in a particular way.

It would now generally be admitted, not least by Moore himself, that the arguments in *Principia Ethica* which purported to give a knock-down proof that good is indefinable do not achieve this end.[5] But his doctrine is plausible. The issue will be clearer when we have considered what the alternative is to something like Moore's view. What will happen if the fundamental concepts of ethics turn out to be all definable in Moore's sense? Of course one ethical concept may be defined in terms of other ethical concepts, but they cannot all be so defined without a vicious circle. If you define A in terms of B and B in terms of A, you will not have given an account which could explain adequately what either term means. Consequently, if all ethical concepts are to be definable, some must be defined in terms of non-ethical concepts, and these will be the fundamental ones. (Those which are definable in terms of other ethical concepts will be not fundamental but derivative from the latter.) But since all ethical concepts must be definable in terms of the fundamental ones, this will reduce the whole content of ethics to something non-ethical. And this is what some of the people whom Moore was criticizing and who have opposed him later have really been doing, whether intentionally or unintentionally.

Let us now consider some of the attempts to define good. For a certain type of mind, very common today, the only tolerable course seems to be to make ethics "scientific" by defining its concepts in terms of the em-

[4] Though we need not act according to the desire we feel most strongly. (*v.* pp. 137-8).

[5] I have not repeated the arguments here for this reason and because of their logical complexity.

pirical concepts of a natural science. Such definitions were described by Moore as naturalistic,[6] and this term has now been generally adopted. In opposition to it a view like Moore's is described as non-naturalist, but one must not regard a non-naturalist view as implying that no senses of "good" can be defined naturalistically. A man might well hold that, when he says "the strawberries are good," he does not mean anything more than that he likes them or possibly that most people would (naturalistic definitions in terms of concepts of psychology), and yet be a non-naturalist because he held that the sense of "good" I have mentioned, the fundamental ethical sense, is not naturalistically definable. Non-naturalism in Ethics must in any case be distinguished from supernaturalism. In denying naturalism Moore did not at all mean to imply that we cannot explain ethics without the introduction of supernatural beings such as a deity. He merely meant to point out the difference between good and the concepts belonging to psychology or any other natural science to which it was sought to reduce good.

Now for the purpose of defining good it is quite obvious at first sight that not every natural science would do. I cannot conceive that anybody in their senses would define the fundamental concepts of ethics in terms of chemistry, geology, botany or astronomy. But there is one science at least in terms of which it is much less unplausible to define ethical concepts, that is, psychology, the science of the human mind, and various attempts have been made to define them in psychological terms.

One proposed way of definition is in terms of approval, by which is meant the unique emotion or emotional attitude that we have when our attention is called to something ethically worthy or admirable. Thus it has been suggested that to say that something is right or good is to say that it is of such a kind as to evoke the approval of most people. But this view is surely open to objections of a very obvious kind. If it were true, it would be self-

[6] This is not Moore's definition, but it represents approximately the way in which the term has been used by him and others.

contradictory to say that a minority who felt disapproval of what most people approved could ever be in the right, and this is surely not so. We cannot possibly say that the majority and not the minority are necessarily right about any particular issue unless we have first considered the issue in question. And how are we to determine what constitutes a majority? It would obviously be arbitrary to confine oneself to people alive at the present time. Why should their ethical sentiments have this supreme authority in determining what is right or good and those of their late parents or grandparents none at all? But, if we took into account everybody who has ever lived, we should have a queer ethics indeed for, taking into account all ages, crude and savage far outnumber tolerably civilized men. And if we included also all future generations, which seems the only consistent course, this would make it impossible save by a miraculous prophecy to determine what is good or right at all. The Earth may continue to be inhabited by men for millions of years, and how are we to tell what the people who inhabit it in those far distant ages will approve or disapprove? Again the mere fact that people disapprove of what I do may make me feel uncomfortable, and if their sentiments are strong enough it may make it highly prudent to change my conduct provided I can do so without going against my conscience, but it could not of itself make it my moral duty to do so. The motive—Seek the approval of others—is not specifically moral: on the contrary it has been recognized by the greatest moral teachers as a major obstacle to true morality. My argument may be put like this—It is obvious that we ought to seek what is intrinsically good or right, just because it is good or right, as the only moral end-in-itself. But it is certainly not the case that we ought to seek what most people approve as the only moral end in itself just because they feel approval of it. Therefore "good" or "right" cannot mean the same as "approved by most people." And I cannot see what point there could possibly be in doing what others would approve if they knew what I have done when in fact they will not know it, unless there is some other reason besides the approval;

yet, if something is my duty, I clearly ought to do it whether others know of it or not. If the approval theory were true, all obligations would be removed by secrecy. But in fact the good man will not value approval except as a sign that he has done something objectively good or right.

Others have attempted a definition in terms not of the approval of most people but of the speaker's own approval, and have maintained that "This is good" or "This is right" means just that the person who uses these words has or tends to have a feeling or attitude of a certain kind about what he pronounces right or good. This view again is open to many objections. Firstly, if this definition were correct, it would follow that a man could never be wrong in an ethical judgement unless he had made a mistake about his own psychology. Again, two people would never mean the same thing when they pronounced an action right or wrong, since either would just mean "It is approved (disapproved) by *me*." Indeed the same person would never mean the same thing by an ethical judgement on two different occasions, since each time he would mean "I *now* feel (or tend to feel) approval of this." Nor, if A pronounced the same action right as B pronounced wrong, would they ever really be in disagreement, for what A would mean is—I (A) feel approval, which is quite compatible with B feeling disapproval at the same time of the same act. Further, when I condemned, e.g. Stalin, I should not be talking about Stalin but only about my own feelings. These consequences would follow if the theory under discussion were true, and they surely constitute a conclusive *reductio ad absurdum* of the theory. And why do I feel approval or disapproval of anything? Surely, normally, because I take it as good or bad, right or wrong independently of my feelings. Also if ethical judgements are simply about our own actual feelings or attitudes, why should we use to support them, as we constantly do, evidence, e.g. about their likely consequences for others, which is certainly not evidence about our own attitudes or feelings?

It has been suggested that ethical concepts should be defined not in terms of people's actual approval but of that of an impartial spectator. But what can "impartial" mean here? Only one who is not influenced in his approvals and disapprovals by circumstances other than those relevant to the real goodness or badness, rightness or wrongness, of what he approves or disapproves. As a definition of an ethical term this is obviously circular. It is equivalent to saying that something is good or right when it is approved by somebody who only approves what is really good or right.

Another psychological concept in terms of which good is sometimes analysed is that of desire or interest (the latter being a wider term used to cover also enjoyment and liking). Thus the important American philosopher, R. B. Perry, has defined good as "object of interest to someone." The reader may be inclined to dismiss this view at once merely on the ground that people sometimes desire evil things, but its defenders would reply that wrongdoing is to be explained not by a man desiring evil for its own sake but by his sacrificing a greater good for a lesser. A thief is not in the wrong because he attaches some value to money, but because he allows his interest in the money to override concern for the rights of others. So it is sometimes argued that all desires are for what is good *per se* and are only bad in so far as they interfere with a greater good. But I cannot see how one can deal in this fashion with the desire for revenge (to inflict pain on another). It may be argued that what the revengeful man really wants is not the pain of his enemy but the pleasure he expects to derive himself from the pain or from the thought of it, but that seems to be committing the fallacy of hedonistic psychology.[7] However, in any case we may object that, if good = desired, better must = desired more, so that the degree of goodness is in proportion to the degree of desire, and this is obviously not so. We all desire the welfare and continued life of those near and dear to us much more than that of people equally worthy, of whom we have just read in the newspaper, and it is certainly not true that most people desire virtue quite as much as they ought to

[7] *v.* above pp. 29-31.

in comparison with other things, e.g. their own happiness or even material welfare. This is just what makes living the good life very difficult for us, and not only intellectually difficult. To say that "good" means "what most people desire" is also open to most of the same type of objections as I have brought against the corresponding theory in terms of approval; and to say that it means what I, the speaker, desire would be to commit oneself to a completely egoistic theory of ethics. Nor can we derive obligation from desire: they are fundamentally different concepts, as we feel when we are convinced that we ought not to do something and yet strongly desire to do it and believe that even its remoter results will be such that we desire them more than those of the action we regard it as our duty to do.

An allied view is that which defines "good" not as "what is actually desired" but as "such as to satisfy our desires in the long run." This again raises difficulties as to degrees of goodness. "The better" would have to be that which satisfies more, and this would practically commit one to hedonism, a view which we have already seen good reason to reject and which is even less satisfactory as a definition of good than as a theory of ethics. If this were the definition, it would be not only false but actually self-contradictory to say that anything could be good except in proportion to the pleasure it gave. A further objection is this. Supposing the definition is understood as referring only to the desires of the individual who pronounces something good, "good" becomes "what will satisfy *me*," and we are again committed to a completely egoistic theory of ethics; if on the other hand the reference is to the desires of people in general, what reason is there for me to seek to satisfy these except in so far as I desire to, unless we introduce the further concept of obligation which cannot be analysed in terms of desire? "I ought to do so-and-so" cannot be identified with "so-and-so is an efficient means towards the general satisfaction of people's desires," for it is certainly not a self-contradictory position for a man to be convinced that he ought to do something and yet doubt whether it is a more efficient means to this than some alternative action which he thinks he ought not to do. E.g. it is not self-contradictory to hold both that I should satisfy more people's desires more fully if I did not p y my debts but did something else with the money and yet hold that I ought to pay my debts. Many desires of others we indeed ought not to try to satisfy, and that most human desires could not be in this position certainly cannot be deduced from a mere definition of good or ought.

In view of the fact that people desire many things which they would not desire if they knew what the attainment of them would involve, it has been suggested that "good" means, not what is actually desired, but what all men would desire if they knew its true nature.[8] However, it is by no means a certainty that all men would desire what is good in proportion to its goodness even if they knew the true nature of the good things in question, but on the contrary at best a highly conjectural proposition. It is by no means certain that Hitler would have desired happiness for Jews as much as for equally worthy Aryans even if he had known how much they suffered through being confined in concentration camps and what was their exact psychological nature. Yet that he would must follow verbally if the definition be correct and we grant that their happiness is of equal value. We may go further and say that none of us would even with the fullest knowledge always desire what was good in proportion to its goodness, since we all inevitably desire the welfare of those we know and love more than that of those who are little more than names to us, though this need not necessarily lead to our sacrificing the latter to the former since we can control our desires for the sake of what is right. This statement about desire surely applies even to the greatest saints. For a man to desire the good of all other men fully as much as an equivalent amount of good for himself or those closest to him it would be necessary, not only that he should know all the circumstances including the state of their feelings, but that his emotional nature should be completely different from ours so that human love as we

[8] *v.* Field, *Moral Theory,* Chap. XI.

know it either did not exist in him at all or was extended equally to everybody. And if we imagine our nature thus completely and superhumanly or inhumanly altered, we can no longer have any foundation for saying what we should desire. In any case it is surely obvious that to call anything good is not to say what would happen if some quite impossible psychological revolution were effected in us.

I have said that of naturalistic definitions of the fundamental ethical concepts psychological are the least unplausible, but definitions in terms of biology and sociology have also been attempted, though these are clearly at the best definitions of instrumental rather than of intrinsic good. Thus biologists or people much influenced by biology have sometimes defined the good or the right as what tends to further human survival. But in ethics we do not aim only at mere life, and though some virtues and vices are likely appreciably to affect the duration of life or the number of descendants produced this is not the case with most. It would follow from the definition that it did not matter how miserable one made anybody else, provided only the misery did not actually shorten his life or diminish the number of his descendants or the chance of his having descendants. It would be better, both hedonistically and morally, not to live at all than to live in the way in which many people have lived. Life in itself is valueless, whether it is good or evil depends on the specific nature of the life in question.

Another biological definition proffered of good or right is "in conformity with evolutionary development." This at once raises difficulties about defining evolution or development. For it may be retorted that everything that happens, good or bad, is in accord with evolutionary development, otherwise it could not happen at all. If, on the other hand, we define evolutionary development as change for the better, as one is tempted to do, the definition of good proposed will constitute a vicious circle. "Good" cannot be defined as "what is in conformity with good development." What is commonly meant seems to be that the good is what is in accordance with the main actual trends in the past and will conduce to similar developments in the future. This avoids the charge that the definition makes everything good, for we can recognize a distinction between the main trends and exceptions which are not characteristic of or actually hinder the predominant line of change. But to say that such and such is an accord with the main trend of development and to say that it is good is surely to say two quite different things. That things should change on the whole in such and such a way is quite compatible with the change being evil and not good. One of the main trends in human development has been that people have shown more and more efficiency in destroying each other in war. Does it follow that it would be good for this process to continue? The same type of consideration applies to other interpretations of the evolutionary definition of good. "Evolved" might mean just "later in time," in which case the definition would involve the unfounded and unreasonable dogma that all change is progress. Or it might mean "more complex," but we surely do not need any argument to determine that goodness is not the same as complexity.

Similar objections apply to the sociological definitions of "good" or "right" as "what furthers the development of society" or "what makes for social stability." What furthered the development of Nazi society and made for its stability was not good but bad. We can only defend the former definition if we already include good in the notion of development thus committing a vicious circle, and the latter if we are prepared to maintain that there is never any value in change and the right course is always simply to maintain the existing form of society.

To each of these naturalist theories there are, as we have seen, very serious specific objections, but there are also general arguments which can be used to rule out on principle any naturalist definition whatever. I mention three. (1) Any naturalist definition would have the effect of reducing ethics to a branch of an empirical science, whether psychology or some other, and this is indeed a great attraction at the present day when "scientific" and "rational" are commonly regarded as synonyms. Yet there is a logical consequence which few would really be prepared to swallow. If ethics is an empirical science, its method must be that of empirical generalization, i.e. as the logician calls it, induction. In order to establish ethical conclusions all that is needed will be to provide, in the case of theories which define ethical concepts in terms of the psychology of the speaker, a few introspections, and in the case of other naturalist theories a set of statistics about the actual feelings or desires of human beings, and these will *ipso facto* settle what is good or right beyond the possibility of contradiction. But this is not at all the method we follow in order to arrive at ethical conclusions, on the contrary it strikes us as in itself completely irrelevant to these. The mere fact that people actually feel in a certain way does not by itself convince us of the truth of anything in ethics, though it may well be a premiss which sometimes together with others leads to a true and reasonable ethical conclusion. No set of statistics by itself, it is surely obvious, can prove an ethical conclusion.[9] We may go even further in our criticism: not only would it follow from naturalism that the truth of ethical propositions was always completely determinable by observations of oneself or sets of statistics about others, it would follow, at least from the forms of naturalism which do not equate ethical propositions with propositions merely about the psychology of the speaker, that all ethical propositions were themselves merely vague propositions about statistics. For the only difference between the proposition "Most people do . . ." and the proposition "91.7% do" is that the former is a very vague and the latter a more precise proposition about statistics. Yet it is surely not true that ethical propositions are propositions about statistics at all, whether precise or vague.

(2) When a definition BC is offered of A, it is plainly a fatal refutation of the definition if we can point to something of which it would be true to say that it is A but false to say that it is BC or vice versa, and I have used objections of this kind against the naturalist theories. But it is

[9] *v.* Broad, *Five Types of Ethical Theory,* pp. 114-5.

an important logical point that in order to refute a definition it is not necessary to show this much. If we can show it to be even possible that it might be true of something that it was A but false that it was BC or vice versa, it is enough to overthrow the definition. For, if BC really were what A meant, it would be self-contradictory to suggest even that A could possibly apply to something and BC not or vice versa, as it would be self-contradictory to suggest that a man could be a father (except in a metaphorical sense) without being a male parent. Thus, even if it were a fact that we always desire what is good and what is good alone, the corresponding definition of good in terms of desire could still be refuted by pointing out that, even if this be in fact true, there would be no contradiction in supposing it false. Even if it be a fact, it must still be admitted that it is just an empirical fact about human nature which might for anything we can see have been quite different, and not something which follows verbally from a knowledge of the way in which we use the term "good." An argument of this type is advanced against all naturalist definitions of "good." With any one we can on inspection see that the property given in the definition might without any contradiction be supposed to belong to something that was not good, and that therefore it cannot be an adequate definition. It is probably this point which Moore had mainly in mind in his attack on naturalism in *Principia Ethica*, and fundamentally it seems to me justified, though his way of putting his case is, as he would be the first to admit, open to criticism. Whatever empirical property is put forward as constituting a definition of "good" (or, for that matter, "obligatory" or "right") it seems clear that the question whether everything that is good (or obligatory or right) has that property or vice versa is not a question of definition at all, and therefore the alleged definition must each time be dismissed as untenable.

(3) A general defect in all naturalist theories is that they do not leave any room for the concept of ought as distinct from what in fact is the case. They all analyse ethical propositions in a way which has reference solely to

what is, but what is is very different from what ought to be. And the sharp transition from the is to the ought they in no wise explain. This objection, used by the philosopher Hume[10] against a very different type of theory, namely, that which deduced ethics from metaphysics, may equally be turned against the naturalism to which Hume himself was inclined. At least a very important feature appertaining to the characteristic of goodness is that it puts people under obligations. If something is good and there is no stronger counter-obligation, we *ought* to promote or at least not destroy it. But not one of the characteristics I have mentioned as equated by various naturalists with goodness seems of itself to carry with it this power to put people under an obligation. If so, none of them can be equated with the characteristic of goodness, which does carry with it this power. No doubt we ought to satisfy the desires of other people, but only in so far as these desires are good; no doubt we ought to do what others approve of our doing, but only in so far as they approve what is right. On no view will the better object always coincide with what I desire more at the time, and even if it did, this would only make it prudent to pursue it rather than the worse, not obligatory; so the question arises why I ought to pursue it, unless it is seen to be self-evident that I ought to pursue the better rather than the worse, as is claimed by the non-naturalist. But if "good" means merely what most people desire or approve, it is by no means self-evident that we ought to pursue it, unless we make it verbally so by defining "I ought to do B" as meaning something like "B is of all actions open to me at the time the best fitted to satisfy men's desires or win their approval," and in that case we are open to the objection that it is impossible to see how we can reduce the notion of ought to what is merely a factual causal connection. A proposition affirming ethical obligation surely cannot merely state that such and such a case produces in fact such and such effects. That is a totally different proposition. These objections apply to all naturalistic theories of ethics.

[10] *Treatise of Human Nature* III, i., I., *ad fin.*

It indeed seems to me that the non-naturalist is in a stronger position against his opponent if he makes his defence centre on the notion of an indefinable "ought" than if he like Moore makes it centre on an indefinable "good." Grave doubts have been expressed as to whether we really are aware of this alleged indefinable quality of goodness, and I myself share these doubts, but it is much more difficult to doubt that we are aware of obligation and that obligation is not reducible to any empirical quality or relation. Once we have admitted an indefinable ought, we may define "good" in its specifically ethical senses by means of this notion. We can then say that to assert something to be intrinsically good is to say that it is "such that we ought to have a favourable attitude towards it, i.e. choose, desire, pursue, further, welcome or admire it, for its own sake," and define a good man (morally) as "one who does what he ought." It is therefore wrong to suppose that the doctrine that good is indefinable is the only alternative to naturalism. We may maintain instead the indefinability of ought. There are indeed three alternatives. (*a*) We may make good indefinable and define ought in terms of it, i.e. we may say that "I ought to do A" means something such as "of the acts in my power at the time A would produce the greatest good." (*b*) We may hold that good and ought are both indefinable. (*c*) We may regard ought as indefinable and define good in terms of ought.[11] Moore took the first view in *Principia Ethica*, but the second in his later work *Ethics*, and the second view is now I think the most common among non-naturalists. Moore's arguments do not seem to be even directed to showing that good is the only indefinable ethical concept, or that good cannot be given a non-naturalist definition in terms of another concept of ethics.

It is a very sound rule, especially in philosophy, that we should, when confronted with a view which seems to us thoroughly unplausible and unreasonable, ask why it seemed plausible to anybody, and I had better ask this

---

[11] It is not of much significance whether "right" or "ought" is used for this purpose. cf. p. 15.

now about naturalism in Ethics. It seems to me that the following reasons largely explain why philosophers have often been tempted to adopt it. (1) It makes ethics into an empirical science, and empirical science has been so immensely successful in providing us with knowledge about the nature of things that it is plausible to suppose that it could be used to discover everything that may be discovered by us at all. But it may be objected that it does not follow that the methods which have been so successful in determining questions of empirical fact will be suitable for answering the, at least *prima facie*, very different questions of ethics.

(2) A non-naturalist view involves the introduction of a quality (good) or a relation (obligation) which is radically different from any other quality or relation and certainly from any which occur in our ordinary empirical knowledge. It was therefore tempting to try to explain away these concepts by analysing them in terms of qualities or relations of a more ordinary type. But, though it is tempting to reduce all knowledge to one type, we have no right to assume dogmatically that it really is of one type. We cannot tell in advance of trying whether the attempt so to reduce it will succeed or fail, and we have no right for the sake of a simplicity, which we do not know to be possible, to explain away real differences. We can always make things simpler by ignoring inconvenient facts, but it is the reverse of scientific to ignore facts. We must be empirically minded, but our ethical experience is just as much experience as is our perception of physical things.

(3) There is a tendency to make the assumption that some definition is needed of our ethical concepts. But, as I have shown, it is clear that everything cannot be defined in the sense of being reduced to something else, and if any concepts are indefinable at all it is only reasonable to suppose that the fundamental concepts of ethics will be so, since otherwise ethics will be reduced without residuum to what is not ethical. We must remember that to say they are indefinable is merely to say that they cannot be reduced to anything else, not that nothing more can be said about them.

(4) It is argued that, if there really were an indefinable quality of goodness perceivable by us, it is incredible that there should be so much dispute about it. Almost everybody would, it might be expected, know what it was, as everybody (except the colour-blind) knows what yellow is. But there are equal difficulties about seeing how, if the term is really definable, there can be such wide divergencies as to the definition or as to whether there is a definition. Of the naturalists themselves two are rarely agreed on the same definition. Yet a correct definition should give us what we mean, and how is it that there should be such widely different views not only as to what is true but as to what we mean by some of the most common terms? This is a difficulty, not as yet completely solved, that arises with all philosophical definition of common terms, and not only in ethics, but at any rate it seems to hit both sides equally. I must add that it seems to me much easier to be sure that we have a clear idea of obligation distinct from desire, fear, emotion or any other psychological terms than that we have a clear idea of an indefinable quality of goodness.

(5) An influential argument for naturalism is that we can explain the origin of ethical ideas and beliefs psychologically from the non-ethical. Both in the life of the individual and the evolution of mankind ethical consciousness must have somehow developed from a state in which there were no ethical ideas or beliefs whatever, so if we are to have a causal explanation of its origin at all, it must be derived from what is not ethical, and various attempts have been made thus to derive it. This line of approach has been supported by the theories of Freud, who in explaining mental ill-health made great use of an irrational sense of guilt derived from punishments and threats in the days of childhood now forgotten as far as the conscious mind is concerned but persisting in their effects on the unconscious. But there are three points to remember here.

(*a*) A thing is not identical with its causes: it does not follow that, because A was brought into existence by B and C, it can possess no qualities except those belonging to B and C. If the psychological theory of the origin of ethical ideas merely tells us what experiences preceded their formation, it is innocuous; but if it therefore claims to analyse the ideas in terms of these non-ethical experiences, it is open to the objections brought against naturalism. If it is true that ethical knowledge in human beings originated from a state in which there was no ethical knowledge, it is equally true that mathematical knowledge originated from a state in which there was no mathematical knowledge, yet this does not reduce it to the experience of number which an ape or very primitive savage has, or the experience we had when we first learnt sums with the help of beads without seeing how the conclusions followed. It is quite possible and reasonable to suppose that primitive non-mathematical and non-ethical experiences eventually brought about the development of a state of mind in which men first had insight into elementary truths in mathematics and ethics, granting they had the capacity for development and rationality. Philosophers have argued that the non-rational could not of itself produce the rational, but if that argument is valid, the conclusion should be that we are ultimately dependent on a rational being (God) who controls the whole evolutionary process, not the patently false one that we are now in no degree rational, or the incredible one that rational beings developed without any cause. As we have emerged from a state in which we could not see that 5×7 is equal to 35, so we have emerged from a state in which we could not see that anything was really wrong but only feel the pain and fear of punishment into a state in which we possess this insight, and the fact that we have it now cannot possibly be disproved by the fact that we did not have it at some time in the past. The theory under discussion is sometimes used to convey the suggestion that ethical ideas are in some way illusory, but if there is a difficulty this would be no remedy for it, since, whether illusory or veridical, they are equally different from their antecedents and so equally difficult to explain by these. An idea is the same idea whether true or false; to make it illusory is not to make it intrinsically more like the factors which gave rise to it.

(*b*) The success of Freud in explaining many psychological phenomena by his theory, and in particular throwing light on a good many cases of morbid guilt, by no means proves that all sense of guilt, still less of obligation, is to be explained by the kind of causes he suggests. Human nature being fallible, any general idea like guilt which we possess is sure to be applied wrongly to some things; any emotion widely felt is sure to be felt sometimes towards objects to which it is not a suitable response, and Freud may perhaps have provided a good explanation of many of these mistakes. But success in explaining particular morbid phenomena does not prove a theory to be also a complete explanation of all healthy development. The sense of guilt has to exist before it can be misapplied, and Freud's work itself is a tribute to its great psychological importance. That it cannot be adequately explained as originating from fear of external punishment is shown by Freud's very insistence that it leads a man actually to seek punishments for himself.

(c) Anybody who uses this line of approach to support a naturalistic analysis of our present ethical judgements must remember that the moral psychology of young children and primitive peoples is among the most obscure and speculative of studies. As Professor Broad says, "Of all branches of empirical psychology that which is concerned with what goes on in the minds of babies must, from the nature of the case, be one of the most precarious" for the simple reason that "babies, while they remain such, cannot tell us what their experiences are."[12] And there are no peoples now surviving who are at nearly so primitive a stage as that in which man first developed ethical ideas, so that we cannot, even precariously, argue from men's conduct to their experiences at this stage. If we discard our clear convictions as to what our present ethical statements mean on account of a theory about the ethics of children or primitive savages, we are rejecting what should be fairly certain on account of what is very uncertain indeed.

The naturalist has, however, a further line of defence

[12] *Mind,* vol. LIII, no. 212, p. 354.

on which he can fall back. He may admit that a naturalistic analysis of what we mean by our ethical terms has been shown to be impossible, but take this as proving only that our ethical judgements, because not susceptible of such an analysis, are all mistaken, and that the task of the moral philosopher is to substitute for these mistaken judgements new ones couched exclusively in naturalistic terms like desire, which, because they have eliminated any trace of an "ought" or "good" that cannot be reduced to the concept of a natural science, in other words, everything specifically ethical, may claim to be true. This sceptical view about ethics is hard to refute conclusively, but harder still to believe. I cannot possibly help believing that I am not mistaken in holding that it would be ethically wrong of me to hire a gang of toughs in order to beat up the first critic who expressed disagreement with my views, and I suspect that, if I did this, he also, however sceptical in theory in his Ethics, would find it very hard to believe that my action was not ethically wrong. Hence naturalism would be much more plausible and attractive if it could be maintained that it gave an account of what we actually mean in our ethical judgements. In that case we could avoid being sceptics in ethics and yet be naturalists, for we could then still say that the judgements of commonsense ethics are often true. But if, as I have tried to show, any naturalistic account of what we assert in our ethical judgements is mistaken, we must choose between being ethical sceptics and giving up naturalism.[13]

We should note that to say that ethical ideas cannot be reduced without residuum to terms which figure in psychology is not to say that they are applicable to anything outside the realm of psychology. With the very doubtful exception of beautiful objects the concept of value cannot be applied to physical things in the sense of intrinsically good, and certainly the more specifically ethical concepts cannot. But to say that value concepts and ethical judgements can be applied only to psychological entities is not

---

[13] For ethical scepticism, *v.* also above p. 26 ff. and below p. 109 ff.

to say that these concepts and judgements are themselves analysable in terms of psychology. It does not follow that ethical judgements state merely that the person who makes the judgement or people in general have a certain psychological attitude, which is what the naturalist means.

I have dealt with naturalism at length because of its popularity, especially in scientific circles, but most philosophers who are naturalistically inclined have, in this country at least, discarded it for a more subtle theory with which I shall deal in the next chapter. However, before going on to this, I have a word to say about a quite different way of defining ethical concepts, that is, in terms of metaphysics. A metaphysical definition is a definition by reference to the ultimate nature of the real as distinguished from the less ultimate aspect in which reality is conceived as appearing for natural science. Of metaphysical definitions we need only trouble about one here, which is by far the clearest and the best known. I refer to the attempt to define ethical concepts in terms of religion by maintaining that to say something is good or right is to say that it is commanded by God. At first sight it may well seem that such a theory is refuted at once by the mere fact that agnostics and atheists can make rational judgements in ethics, but it will be replied that what even the atheist really has in mind when he thinks of obligation is some confused idea of a command, and that a command implies a commander and a perfect moral law a perfectly good commander on whose mind the whole moral law depends, so that the atheist is inconsistent in affirming the validity of the moral law and yet denying the existence of God. It may be doubted whether this argument, if valid, would make the theological statement an analysis of what the man meant and not rather of the logical consequences of what he meant, but there are other objections to such a definition.

(*a*) If "right" and "good" are themselves defined in terms of the commands of God, God cannot command anything because it is right or good, since this would only mean that He commanded it because He commanded it, and therefore there is no reason whatever for His commands, which become purely arbitrary. It would follow that God might just as rationally will that our whole duty should consist in cheating, torturing and killing people to the best of our ability, and that in that case it would be our duty to act in this fashion.

(*b*) And why are we to obey God's commands? Because we ought to do so? Since "we ought to do A" is held to mean "God commands us to do A," this can only mean that we are commanded by God to obey God's commands, which supplies no further reason. Because we love God? But this involves the assumptions that we ought to obey God if we love Him, and that we ought to love Him. So it again presupposes ethical propositions which cannot without a vicious circle be validated by once more referring to God's commands. Because God is good? This could only mean that God carries out His own commands. Because God will punish us if we do not obey Him? This might be a very good reason from the point of view of self-interest, but self-interest cannot, as we have seen, be an adequate basis for ethics. Without a prior conception of God being good or His commands being right God would have no more claim on our obedience than Hitler except that He would have more power to make things uncomfortable for us if we disobeyed Him than Hitler ever had, and that is not an ethical reason. A moral obligation cannot be created by mere power and threat of punishment. No doubt if we first grant the fundamental concepts of ethics, the existence of God may put us under certain obligations which we otherwise would not have had, e.g. that of thinking of God, as the existence of a man's parents puts him under certain obligations under which he would not stand if they were dead, but we cannot possibly derive all obligations in this fashion from the concept of God. No doubt, if God is perfectly good, we ought to obey His will, but how can we know what His will for us is in a particular case without first knowing what we ought to do?

What I have said of course constitutes no objection to the belief in God or even to the view that we can have a valid argument from ethics to the existence of God, but these views can be held without holding that our ethical terms have to be defined in terms of God. It has been held that the existenc ¬f anything implies the existence of God, but it would not therefore be concluded that the meaning of all our words includes a reference to God. Nor is what I have said meant to imply that religion can have no important bearing on ethics, but I think its influence should lie more in helping people to bring themselves to do what would be their duty in any case and in influencing the general spirit in which it is done than in prescribing what our duty is. While it is quite contrary to fact to suggest that an agnostic or atheist cannot be a good man, the influence in the former respects of religious belief, whether true or false, cannot be denied to have been exceedingly strong.

Metaphysical definitions, like naturalistic, err in trying to reduce the "ought" to the "is." Like them they would destroy what Kant calls the autonomy of ethics by refusing to recognize the uniqueness of its fundamental concepts and trying to reduce it to a mere branch of another study, in this case not a natural science but metaphysics or theology. The theological definition is more ethical than naturalism only in so far as it covertly reintroduces the notion of obligation or goodness thus involving a vicious circle. Indeed it is only plausible because God is already conceived as good. Apart from this it would make duty consist just in obeying the stronger, for if you once exclude the specifically ethical element from the conception of the Deity, God has no claim on us except that of mere power. But it cannot be *morally* obligatory to obey some being just because he is powerful. Let us now turn to consider a second line of approach by which naturalistically inclined philosophers have tried to avoid the kind of position defended in this chapter.

See Notes to Chapters 6 and 7 on pp. 156-57.

Chapter 7

The Nature of Ethical "Judgement"

THE TERM *judgement,* I should begin by saying, is used by philosophers as a convenient term to cover cases both of knowledge and of belief. A judgement should be distinguished from the words used to express it and still more from the outward expression to other people of what is judged, being a mental thought or act, which may be carried out in silence, though hardly without using words to oneself, and consists in seeing that something is true or in deciding to accept something as true. What is thus affirmed as true, as distinguishable from the words in which it is expressed, is called by contemporary philosophers a *proposition*. But we have now to deal with a view which, paradoxically enough, denies that there are any ethical propositions at all.

The question which I shall mainly discuss in this chapter is raised by certain philosophers who are naturalistically inclined. They meet the objections to naturalism by admitting that a naturalistic analysis cannot give an adequate account of our ethical judgements, but insisting that what is left over is not anything that could be true or false but a mere expression of the attitude of the speaker.[1] Now in maintaining this view they have indeed fastened on a very important aspect of the ethical judgement. It is not a purely theoretical or intellectual matter; it does not merely state that something is the case and leave it at that. It is practical, its main function being to urge others or to screw ourselves up to do or abstain from doing something which it occurs to us might be done. And some philosophers would either stop here and say that it communicates no truth at all but only expresses an emotional and practical attitude, or limit the truths it communicates

[1] The best-known expositions of this view are given by Ayer in *Language, Truth and Logic* (1936) chap. VI, and in much greater detail by C. L. Stevenson, in *Ethics and Language* (1944).

to empirical, psychological truths about our own and other people's attitudes, while insisting that what is distinctively ethical is not the communication of these truths but the way in which the emotions of oneself and others are stimulated by this process as an incentive or inhibitor of action. Such a theory explains, it is claimed, why any naturalistic account appears inadequate, for a naturalistic account, they say, at best gives only that element in ethical judgements which can be true or false, and this leaves aside the main part of the moral attitude altogether, which is not cognitive at all but emotional and practical. "Ethical judgements," it is held, are *toto genere* different from judgements as to matters of empirical fact, but they do not differ, as the non-naturalist holds, in asserting something which is not an empirical fact but some other kind of fact; they differ in that either they do not assert facts at all or that, if they do, this is only a relatively unimportant part of their function. We can thus deny that "ethical judgements" are essentially judgements of natural science without accepting a non-naturalist view, for we can say they are not really judgements at all or not primarily so, it being certainly an essential characteristic of judgement to assert what can be true or false. Strictly speaking, a person who holds this view has no right to speak of "ethical *judgements*" at all since he denies their existence but to cover this position and avoid inconvenience I shall continue to use the phrase in inverted commas to signify those experiences, apparently but according to some not really like judgements, which we have when we evaluate or make moral decisions.

What they are if they are not really judgements it is more difficult to say. They have sometimes been described as "commands," but this will not do. I may command you to do something without ever thinking that you ought to do it, and there must always be an additional, specifically ethical reason before we can say that anybody morally ought to obey a command. For the same reason we cannot identify them with "persuasions" or "exhortations," milder terms allied to "commands." I might persuade a person to do things which we both believed to be wrong, by using prudential as opposed to moral grounds or by sheer rhetoric or force of personality. Further, it would have to be admitted that ethical judgements have not just one function but quite a variety depending on the context and the purpose of the speaker. But certainly an "ethical judgement" expresses an attitude of some sort which transcends the purely theoretical when it has a reference to present or future action. It is not so clear that it has a practical reference when the judgement is about an act already done, but even here it may be argued that we are not merely saying something about the nature of the act but taking up an emotional attitude towards it and enjoining or urging others to do the same. We are not merely saying that it was so-and-so, we are approving, welcoming, admiring or deploring, rejecting, condemning it. And when the reference is to "good" instead of "right," we are taking up these attitudes relatively to certain ends or relatively to a type of character. To approve something is not just to assert a proposition, to make an intellectual judgement about it; it is to adopt a positive emotional attitude favouring it, to set ourselves to support it or anything like it (except in so far as our sentiment should be overruled in the future by other considerations).

It has been insisted again and again in recent times, especially by thinkers of this type, that the function of language is not merely to make assertions, but also to express emotional attitudes and urge others to action. This applies also to many theoretical statements about matters of fact, e.g. those made in political disputes. It has even been contended that all judgements without exception have an "emotive" element, as it is called; but while this, if present at all, is negligible in at least very many factual judgements, e.g. most of those made in a geographical text-book, it is obviously of much greater importance in "ethical judgements."

But are we to go further and say that "ethical judgements" do not assert anything at all? It is a matter of common knowledge that we often use sentences which do not make an assertion and so cannot be called true or false but fulfil only the functions of expressing our state of mind and inducing others to act in a certain way. Exclamations, wishes, commands, exhortations come under this head; and it is contended in certain quarters that what we call ethical judgements, while not exactly like any of these, resemble all four more than they resemble factual judgements and in particular resemble them in *asserting* nothing. For, even if we can analyse ethical judgements in such a way as to include in them factual assertions about psychology, e.g. about one's own feelings, the essentially ethical element is still left out when we have enumerated these. On this the holders of the view under discussion seem to be in agreement with the non-naturalists, only they differ in that, while the latter think this element to consist in the assertion of truths of a non-empirical kind, the former do not think that it consists in any assertion at all but in an expression of attitude. There remains for them the problem of distinguishing psychologically the kind of emotional attitudes expressed in "ethical judgements" from non-ethical kinds. They do not usually claim to have achieved complete success in this, but one important difference they have emphasized is that in "ethical judgements" we want our attitude shared by everybody else in so far as we are ethical. (We might of course well want it not to be shared by others for non-ethical reasons, e.g. to escape punishment or general disapproval for ourselves.)

What is the function of ethical argument on this view? It cannot be denied that arguments, including reference to empirical facts quite extraneous to the speaker's own feelings, play a very large part in ethics and are constantly of great importance in determining a person's ethical decisions. But how can "ethical judgements" be supported or refuted by arguments if they do not assert anything? In reply to this objection it is suggested that what happens is not that the ethical arguments adduced show any ethical conclusion to be true or probable, but merely that they often serve to put the person who hears them in such a state of mind that he will adopt the attitude desired by the speaker. Thus, while the argument that a proposed act would hurt somebody very greatly without any corresponding advantage does not on this view show the act to be wrong, it does commonly put people into a state of mind in which they will feel disapproval of it and so will be less inclined to do it.

This view is obviously liable to several of the objections brought against the view that "ethical judgements" are assertions about the attitude of the speaker.[2] To the argument that it would follow that two such "ethical judgements" could never contradict each other its advocates reply that, while they could not contradict each other logically since neither claims to be true, they still contradict each other in an important sense, namely, the sense in which two incompatible aims or policies conflict. But this is a quite different sense of "contradiction," and it is very hard to believe that they contradict each other only in the latter sense and not in the former. To bring this out, let us take the illustration of two candidates, A and B, competing for the same post or trying to buy tickets to a performance when these are almost all sold. Their attitudes or aims conflict, but this is very different from saying that there is any logical contradiction between judgements made by them. Neither need judge that he is the better man for the post or that it would be better that he should have a ticket rather than the other, and therefore there need be no incompatible judgements involved. But the situation seems quite different when A says that something ought and B that it ought not to be done. Then they seem plainly not merely to be opposing each other in action and policy but to be each saying something which the other judges false.

It seems to me clear that both the extreme types of views, the purely intellectualist one and the one I have just outlined, overlook one side of the situation, but I think the error of those who deny that "ethical judgements" are really judgements is a much more serious one. As a matter of fact it may be doubted whether a purely intellectualist theory is held by anyone. We, non-naturalist writers, may be open to criticism in that we did not say

[2] *v.* above p. 84.

enough about the emotive and practical function of "ethical judgements," but none of us denied that they had such a function, and I cannot imagine anybody who understands what the words mean doing so. The only main question at issue is whether they have also what is called a cognitive function, i.e. whether they also make assertions which can be called true or false. It is only too obvious that they commonly express and evoke emotions and stimulate to action and that they are made largely for these purposes.

To settle the question of the nature of "ethical judgements" what is called for is a careful examination of our state of mind in making them. This examination each reader should conduct for himself and not leave only to me. For my part I must confess to a suspicion that many people who have expressed their views on the subject have neglected to carry out the examination because they assumed that there could not be any valid or even any meaningful assertions outside the sphere of natural science, but they cannot possibly prove any such thing, and they have no right just to assume this *a priori* without examining our ethical experience. Now such an examination seems to me to show clearly that a conviction that something is really objectively good or bad, right or wrong, is normally prior to the more practical and emotional side of the attitude or at least intimately linked up with it, and that without this conviction the attitude is not really ethical but simply a matter of taste or unethical preference. (I do not mean of course hereby to accuse people who reject any objective view of being unethical, but only of having interpreted their experience wrongly.) Let anyone in doubt about this question look at the process of making up one's mind whether a particular action is right as distinct from the (alas!) different process of deciding to do it. Making up one's mind what one ought to do is surely asking a question and trying to find out the true answer. This is brought out especially when we consider what we are doing when we ask for advice. When asking the advice of a friend we do not merely want him to bring us into an emotional state of approval towards a proposed act, or at least if that is all we want, it will be agreed that we are not asking in the right spirit but merely wishing to feel comfortable about the action. Nor is it merely that we wish him to induce us to perform some act or other as well as give us this feeling of comfort about what we do. If so, again we are not behaving ethically but merely seeking to escape the trouble of decision. We wish him to help us to find out what is really right independently of our state of feeling about it. Even if we accept his opinion simply on authority, this can only be ethically justified, if at all, in cases where we rationally think his ethical opinion more likely to be true than our own. Nor again is it merely that we want to have similar feelings about the action to his. This is probably part of what we want, but if it is all, our motive is certainly not ethical in the least.

And can we really believe that our judgements that, e.g. Hitler acted badly or that the needless infliction of pain on others is wrong do not claim to be true? If the cognitive element were altogether removed, adverse "ethical judgements" would be mere abuse like swear-words used in anger without any claim to rational justification or shouts or threats intended to browbeat or frighten people into doing what we want. There would be no good reason for any "ethical judgement" rather than any other. It is true that the theory tries to leave a place for reasoning in ethics, as we have seen, but its exponents have to admit that no argument can establish or refute any "ethical judgement" or even make it more or less probable, for ethical judgements do not assert anything that could be made true or probable. All "reasoning" can do on their view is to render people more or less liable to make an "ethical judgement." This is to draw no distinction between rational argument in ethics and mere "propaganda": people may be induced to make "ethical judgements" by all sorts of irrelevant circumstances, but it is surely plain that, e.g. the fact that an action would produce suffering is not merely a cause which renders most people disinclined to do it, but a reason which objectively tends in the direction of making the action wrong, whatever people's feelings and attitudes about it. It is a fatal objection to the view we are criticizing, at least as usually stated,[3] that it does not distinguish between actual and right approval. According to it, anybody who says that approvals are right or wrong is still merely expressing his actual attitude of approval or disapproval towards them. In this respect it is in the same position as the naturalist theory which analysed ethical concepts in terms of approvals. For as that theory held that ethical judgements merely assert that people approve, this one holds that they merely express approvals. But surely the least that must be admitted is that in "ethical judgements" we at any rate claim that the attitude we approve emotionally and try to induce others to adopt is justifiable or fitting, i.e. is not merely our actual attitude but the attitude that ought objectively to be adopted by us, and in so far as we are ethical that is just why we feel approval of it and urge others to adopt it. Of course we may easily be mistaken in our claim in particular cases, but are we speaking ethically at all unless we make it?

Of course in the present discussion I am not intending to deny, because I do not mention, the importance of education, but there is no doubt that we may see for ourselves later the truth of what we are first taught on authority. In my analysis of "ethical judgement" I am considering not parrot-like acceptance but intelligent realization and decision. The fact that we were first taught ethics by somebody else need not raise doubts of it in our mind provided we can see ethical truths for ourselves now, unless indeed we are to have similar doubts of mathematics. We may well have acquired an ethical view in the first place merely by accepting it on authority and yet appreciate for ourselves its validity later on in life. After all most people only come to know in the first instance that $5 + 7 = 12$ or that the three angles of an Euclidean triangle are equal to two right angles because their teacher told them so.

In face of the plain evidence to the contrary, how can anyone maintain the view we have criticized? Apart from

[3] But v. below, pp. 118-9.

the ungrounded, though in the historical circumstances understandable, prejudice against whatever cannot be fitted into the rubric of natural science, the people who have done so have been influenced largely by the difficulties involved in deciding whether an ethical judgement is true or false; but the conclusion from this argument, if valid at all, should be not that we do not make ethical judgements in the proper, cognitive sense of "judgement," but that those we make are not justified. Yet, since hardly anybody can really believe that none of our "ethical judgements" are justified, these philosophers have contended that they are justified but that their justification does not lie in their truth, since they have a practical function and do not claim truth or only claim it through a misunderstanding. This seems to me in flagrant conflict with our ethical consciousness, which forces us to insist that our ethical judgements are not justified unless they are true. So I am forced to choose between a complete ethical scepticism, i.e. a denial that any ethical judgements are justifiable, which is a view arguable in a philosophical discussion but impossible to any sane man in ordinary practice, and a view according to which ethical judgements can assert real truths about values and obligations that cannot just be reduced to statements about the actual feelings and attitudes of human beings. Very many ethical judgements are no doubt highly doubtful, but the presumption in favour of the truth of some, e.g. that I ought not to kill the next man I see in order to rifle his pockets, is so strong that it could not possibly be overthrown by any but the most conclusive logical disproof, and on the admission even of the opponent of my view such a conclusive disproof is impossible. If, on the other hand, the sceptic demands for judgements in ethics a logical proof as we have in mathematics or an empirical inductive proof as we have in natural science, he is condemning ethics because ethical judgements have their own distinctive criteria and are not quite like other judgements, which resembles the attitude of the man who should condemn empirical evidence because it is not mathematical or mathematical evidence because it is not empirical.

Plausible-sounding arguments have been advanced not only for ethical scepticism but for scepticism as regards all alleged knowledge and belief, a position which assuredly nobody accepts. Yet the complete theoretical sceptic cannot be refuted any more than the sceptic in ethics, for if he is a complete sceptic he will refuse to accept the premises of any argument against himself or the logical principles underlying the argument in question. There is indeed a close analogy between the two cases: the theoretical sceptic can be logically proved to be inconsistent if he claims truth for anything he says, and in practice even a very sceptically inclined person can hardly avoid doing this, but he cannot be logically refuted if he merely talks without claiming to assert anything true. Similarly the absolute ethical sceptic can be shown inconsistent if he admits explicity or implicitly the truth of any value judgements, and it is almost as difficult to avoid doing this as to be a consistent sceptic in the theoretical field. And just as the theoretical sceptic can still talk, so the sceptic as to values can still act in accordance with his desires (including his moral desires); but as the theoretical sceptic cannot consistently claim that there is any justification for any of his statements, so this other sceptic cannot claim that there is any justification for any of his acts, that any act is more rational than any other possible act. Even prudential and not only moral decisions assume value judgements for their justification, at least the judgement that it is better that oneself should enjoy pleasure than suffer pain.

It remains, however, important for me to deal with the difficulties raised by the widespread differences in ethical belief between different people, which differences may seem to point strongly in the direction of ethical scepticism. The differences are certainly striking enough. Many savages have thought it their duty to practise human sacrifice or to kill their parents when the latter attained a certain age; to come nearer home, in the Middle Ages most Europeans thought it right or even a duty to burn alive those who disagreed with them on certain points of theology, and in the most recent times the differences between the ethical views of Nazis, Communists and Democrats have proved great indeed. Since people differ so enormously in their ethical judgements, the question is raised whether we are entitled to admit any ethical truth anywhere. We must not, however, let a consideration of the differences in ethical beliefs carry us too far. There are also enormous differences between different peoples as to matters of objective fact about the physical world. Are we to conclude that, because primitive peoples believe the earth to be flat and we believe it to be round, that therefore it has no shape at all? Or that there are no true propositions about race because the Nazi account of it differs so much from ours? That would be parallel to saying that, because people differ very much in their ethical judgements, these are therefore neither true nor false. Rival political parties differ usually quite as much in their factual assertions about what caused certain events or what effects certain events will produce as in their judgements about what ought to be done. Are we then to conclude that the events in question have no causes or no effects?

Indeed the majority of ethical differences are due to differences of belief as to matters of fact. Why did the medieval inquisitors think it their duty to burn people alive for their theological beliefs, while I should think it very wicked? Chiefly because they differed from me in holding that in the case of certain beliefs theirs was the only way to save more people from being burnt eternally. Why have savages practised human sacrifice? Chiefly because they thought it to be the only way of stopping pestilences, which we do not. Why in some tribes did the children kill their parents? Either because they thought that, if one lived till old age, one would have to spend the whole of one's future existence with an aged body, or because they thought, perhaps in this case rightly, that they could not procure enough food to maintain them. If we granted the truths of these non-ethical beliefs, it would be at least arguable that the practices were justified. It might indeed be contended that all these terrible things ought not to be done (at least against the will of the people concerned) even if the effects were good, but since most of us approve of doing at least equally terrible things in war if the evils they are supposed to avert are sufficiently great, we are in no position to throw stones at the savages. The ordinary differences too between people in the same community as to what ought to be done turn most commonly on differences of belief as to the consequences of the acts to which the disputes relate. E.g. what are likely to be the effects of telling so-and-so what I think of him? What kind of education is most likely to bring out certain qualities in a child? What will be the ultmate economic effects of a wage increase?

Again, in some cases where there seems to be an ethical difference there is not really one at all since it is not really but only nominally the same act which is in question. For what can be externally classified as the same kind of act, when performed in a society with a different psychology and different institutions, is not really the same. It is obvious that a person might consistently hold war under certain circumstances to be justifiable as practised at some earlier stages of civilization and yet wrong as practised by modern states, for war is quite a different institution according to whether it is carried on by primitive tribes or by modern nation-states. It might without self-contradiction be maintained that slavery and polygamy were right in ancient Egypt and yet wrong in the United States in the nineteenth century A.D. In Egypt these institutions may conceivably have constituted the least harmful way then available to the inhabitants of dealing with the problems of labour and marriage, while in the United States they did not. And with lesser divergencies it must very commonly be the case that both sides are right in the sense that the acts they advocate are each justified in their context and would be recognized by the other party too as justified if he understood the circumstances.

It is not, however, possible to explain all apparent ethical divergencies in these ways. There are no doubt real ethical differences which would remain even if everybody were in agreement about the actual consequences of acts. Some of these may be explained by differences in people's experiences. Even on an objective non-naturalist view we cannot, except on somebody else's authority, decide whether something is intrinsically good unless we have had the experience in question, and even where the physical circumstances or objects experienced are the same the experiences of different people differ. We must remember that what is intrinsically good is not a physical thing or a physical act but the experience or state of mind connected with it. This easily explains how many people may, for instance, profoundly differ as to their evaluation of works of art; and even if philosophy is, as I think, intrinsically valuable, a person will never find it so if he is incapable of or fails to develop any genuine philosophical experience. Again even if we know intellectually that something will hurt another person badly, our opinions as to what is right will be liable not to be sufficiently affected by this knowledge if we are unsympathetic and so fail sufficiently to realize his pain. Other differences as to what is right are due to the application or misapplication by one side or both of principles accepted on authority or to genuine intellectual confusions such as the philosopher or even the man of common sense who is not a philosopher could remove. A very common source of difference of opinion is one-sidedness. The consequences of actions are on any tenable view of ethics at least very relevant to their rightness or wrongness, and these consequences are liable to be mixed. One person will then concentrate his attention on the good ones almost exclusively and so forget or underestimate the evil, while another will likewise forget or underestimate the good. Men have often so concentrated their attention on the unselfish heroism which war brings out that they most grossly underestimated its evils; some (though not all) pacifists have spoken as it if brought out no good at all. We can well avoid the grosser degrees of this one-sidedness and it is one of the most neglected of duties to try sufficiently hard to do so, but it must be realized that in more complicated cases decision is a very difficult matter of balancing good against evil, and the difficulty is to a very large extent due to the need for keeping our attention fairly directed to all the chief relevant circumstances at once. If we fail to do this, we are liable, even when we have forecasted the actual consequences rightly, to attach too much weight to the good or evil in some and too little to that in others (especially the remoter ones).

So it is not at all difficult to explain the differences of opinion on ethical questions without abandoning the view that our ethical judgements claim objective truth and that this claim is often justified. To the sources of error which I have mentioned must of course be added the fact that people often do not want to find out what is right because they consciously or subconsciously fear that they will then have to fulfil a duty which they dislike. Obviously we need not be surprised if people fail to attain a truth that they do not want to find. It should be noted that every one of these sources of error may and very commonly do affect not only ethical beliefs but beliefs as to matters of fact. If so, we cannot use the occurrence of the errors as an argument against the objectivity of ethics unless we are prepared to admit a similar argument against the objectivity of judgements about matters of fact. I have been referring primarily here to differences as to what we ought to do in particular cases; differences between philosophers as to the general theory of ethics are remarkably great, but experience shows that very wide philosophical differences are quite compatible with striking agreement as regards the kind of actions judged right or wrong, just as radical differences between philosophers in their theories of perception and of matter are quite compatible with complete agreement as to the position of the furniture in their rooms. The differences between philosophers are not in the main differences as to their ethical judgements in concrete situations, but as to the general theory explaining these.

We, in fact, find it commonly admitted even by opponents of an objective ethics that the argument from differences of opinion is by no means conclusive. What makes the difficulty worse than it is as regards differences about matters of fact is that in ethics we soon seem driven to fall back on intuitions not susceptible of proof so that there seems no way of deciding rationally between the disputants. But has not what I have just said about ethical differences disclosed various ways in which such disputes may be decided? Clearly, even where there is agreement as to the likely consequences of an action, the disputants may still differ as to whether it ought to be done because they evaluate these differently, but it is not as if there were no rational means of helping to correct evaluations. A may hold a different view from B because he has not turned his attention sufficiently to certain aspects of the consequences; these may be pointed out to him. He again may hold a different view because he is lacking in certain experiences which are needed to appreciate the value (or the reverse) of certain elements in the consequences. Here the solution in practice is more difficult, but in theory the ideal course is to supply him with the missing experiences, and if this is impossible an attempt may be made at least to show him what they mean to other people. There is plenty of scope for tact and sometimes eloquence here. Again, what a person seems to himself to know intuitively may be really an unconscious or half-conscious, and perhaps erroneous, inference, and this may be unmasked and refuted with the result that the alleged intuition disappears. Or there may be a mixture of genuine intuition and intellectual confusion. A man may think that he has an intuition that P is R when he really only knows intuitively that it is Q but confuses Q with R or as the result of an incorrect inference assumes that Q involves R. Clearly these errors can on principle be put right. Other errors are emotional and not intellectual in origin. Of these many will be removed if the person concerned merely makes an honest effort to avoid prejudice; a psychologist will have plenty of methods to suggest by which others could be removed. Further, even if what presents itself intuitively cannot be proved or disproved, inference may be used at least to cast doubt on it or partially to confirm it. Attention may be called in disputed cases to the effects which have accrued in the past from acting on other parallel occasions in a way similar to that proposed now or to the results which would follow if everybody were to adopt the rule of conduct proposed. We may remind a man what he himself thought of somebody else who acted in a manner similar to that in which he intends to act now, in this and other ways appealing to the test of consistency. To take a case of a general principle, our strong intuitive belief in the obligation to keep promises may be confirmed and supported by a realization both of Kant's point that the policy of breaking promises cannot be consistently universalized, and still more, by a consideration of the point that promise-keeping in general is linked with the fulfilment of other *"prima facie"* duties, has good consequences and is essential for the maintenance of an ordered society, i.e. by the coherence of the belief with the results of the application of other ethical criteria. What unnecessarily violates one *prima facie* duty commonly violates others or puts us in a position ultimately in which we cannot help violating another one. What produces one kind of good consequence, e.g. virtue or truth, commonly produces another, e.g. happiness. We must not suppose that, because an intuition is not proved true by reasoning, therefore it cannot be supported by reasoning. The use of tests does not imply that the belief tested is to be based on the tests alone, but the tests and the original intuition tested confirm each other. As I have pointed out earlier,[4] the criterion of the truth of a theory of Ethics is its ability to make into a coherent system as much as possible of our ethical intuitions (common-sense ethics).

There is thus no lack of means available for settling ethical disputes. We shall certainly not always be successful in settling them, but even scientists are not always successful in solving their own problems. It is sufficient to meet attacks on the objectivity of ethics if they are soluble *in principle*, i.e. if we can point to methods by which they could be solved, granting intelligence, good will and open-mindedness on both sides. Even the physical scientist cannot claim more than this for his subject, though the degree of his success in solving problems to the general satisfaction is nowadays much greater. He can produce no foolproof technique usable by everybody for safely settling

---

[4] *v.* above pp. 10-1.

scientific problems (making discoveries); he cannot guarantee that even the most gifted will always be able to think of a crucial experiment by means of which his methods of discovery can be applied to lead to a decisive result, or even that such a crucial experiment will always be physically in our power. All he can say is that he has methods which can on principle solve all scientific problems, if circumstances favour and the human factor comes up to the mark, and we can say as much as this about ethics. We must remember also that physical science has only reached its present proud position after a period of millennia in which the verdict of what passed for science in those days was far less reliable than are most of our ethical judgements. It is certainly no argument against the objectivity of ethics that we cannot solve all ethical problems immediately. Still less is it an argument against it when we fail to settle disputes through unwillingness to make a sufficient effort to dispel our prejudices.

An argument which is sometimes used is that ethics is so very different from science or everyday factual knowledge that "truth" would have to mean something so different as applied to ethics that we ought not to use the same word. I do not accept the contention, for the differences seem to lie not in the meaning of "truth" but in the nature of the subject-matter of these different studies and so in the nature of what is true; but even if it were accepted, what I have said shows at any rate the kinship between right ethical judgements and judgements objectively true in the scientific sense, while admitting a big difference in the methods of determining their validity and in the kind of thing they assert. If a philosopher prefers not to use the word "true" of "ethical judgements" but admits the points which I have made as showing a strong analogy between them and judgements which can be true, the difference between us may be less one of essence than of emphasis. I am inclined to think that the difference between ethical and factual judgements is better expressed by saying that they are quite different kinds of assertions than by saying merely that they introduce a new special kind of property or relation. Yet to say that they are so different that "ethical judgements" are not true or not even judgements seems to me not illuminating, but misleading in a serious degree. The essential point is, however, that even if a thinker has come to prefer not to use the words "true" and "false" in connection with "judgements" of ethics, he must still draw a distinction between actual and right "judgements," so far as to admit that some "ethical judgements," if not true, are at least justifiable, rational, fitting, and others, if not false, irrational, unjustified, unfitting. There is a tendency nowadays in various quarters to insist on the one hand that "ethical judgements" cannot be in the strict sense true just because they are so different from scientific judgements, and on the other, that they yet have a logic of their own and can be based on right or wrong reasons,[5] and this position is far nearer to my own view than are the views I have been criticizing.

The present seems to me a suitable occasion for saying something more about "intuition" and its place in ethics. It is a well-known fact that propositions, particularly in ethics, but also in other fields of thought, sometimes present themselves to a person in such a way that without having even in his own opinion established them by empirical observation or by argument he seems to himself to see them directly and clearly to be true. This is often expressed by saying that he has or at least seems to himself to have an *intuition* of their truth. It might be expressed without using the term *intuition* by saying simply that he knows or rationally believes them to be true without having any reasons or at least seems to himself to do so. Some such intuitions or apparent intuitions are no doubt explicable as due to quick and half-conscious, or even in some sense unconscious, inference, deductive or inductive, but I do not see how we can explain all or even most ethical "intuitions" in this way. For in the absence of a conclusive proof of ethical propositions from non-ethical, which it would take a bold man at the present stage of the development of thought to regard as possible, some ethical propositions must be known immediately if any are to be known

---

[5] e.g. Toulmin, *Reason in Ethics*.

at all. Ethical facts are not the sort of thing that can be discovered by sense-perception, and we can know no ethical truths by argument unless we know the ethical premises to be true. This in the eyes of some people casts suspicion and doubt on the objective truth of ethics, but these doubts will be lessened when it is realized that the need for admitting intuition is by no means confined to ethics. This we can show by a simple logical argument to the effect that some intuition is necessarily presupposed in all reasoning. Suppose I argue A, ∴ B, ∴ C. Now the argument is invalid unless B does really follow from A, but how can I know that it does so? I may be able to interpolate an intermediate proposition D which itself follows from A and from which B follows, but this only puts the problem further back. I must know that D follows from A, and though I might perhaps be able to interpolate a further intermediate stage, I obviously cannot go on in this way *ad infinitum*. Sooner or later, and probably very soon indeed, I must come to some link between A and the next term in the inference which I can see immediately to hold without being able to prove this by further argument. We may take it then that, if we are to have any knowledge by inference, intuitive knowledge must occur, and the same is true if we substitute for "knowledge" in both places "justified (rational) belief." The argument shows that all apparent intuitions cannot possibly be reduced to suppressed inferences, since inference itself presupposes intuition of the connections between the different stages in the inference. Even if we made explicit all the intermediate steps of a suppressed inference, they would never justify our conclusion in the absence of this. Ethical intuitions are not indeed intuitions of logical connections, but at least the present argument shows that, if we are to have inference in any sphere, the possibility of intuition cannot be rejected on principle. The mere fact that intuitions have to be admitted in ethics cannot be made an objection against ethics, since it has been shown that we have also to admit intuition with all knowledge outside ethics that involves inference. The term intuition is apt to be suspect, but to say somebody knows something intuitively is only to say that he knows it otherwise than by simple observation or reasoning.

Now when we examine the nature of our ethical thought on its own merits, we do find that it presupposes certain ethical truths which we must know intuitively or not at all. For instance, we object to a man doing something because, we say, it is unkind, meaning that it will cause unnecessary pain to others. But why should he not cause unnecessary pain to others if he so desires? Our objection that he ought not to do so presupposes that pain is evil, and that we ought not unnecessarily to inflict evil on other men. I do not see how these truths can be proved: they are known intuitively, if at all. And in general it is very hard to see how we can know anything to be intrinsically good or bad except by intuition. What argument could prove it? Yet nothing can be really good or bad in the instrumental sense unless it can produce what is intrinsically good or bad, so that ethics is at a complete standstill without knowledge of the latter. I think, however, that both in the development of the individual and of the race particular intuitions come first and general ones later: we saw the evil of a particular pain before we generalized and said that pain was evil, but once we have made the generalization we can without having to prove it see it to be true.

Intuitions also seem to be necessarily present in ethical judgement when we consider the final stage in which we after estimating the factual consequences see or judge an act to be right or wrong. For we have to balance the good and evil in the consequences against each other,[6] and there are no rules of logic or calculations of mathematics by which we can do that. We just see that one set of consequences or one act is preferable to a suggested alternative after having viewed them as a whole, paying attention to their relevant factual aspects. The points we adduce on either side do not prove (except in simple cases) that an act is right or wrong, but rather put us in a position in which we have more chance of seeing whether it is right or wrong.

[6] And, on one view, our *prima facie* duties apart from the good or evil liable to be produced.

Most philosophical defenders of intuition have preferred not to use the word except in cases where they claimed certain knowledge. But at any rate we must admit that people sometimes seem to themselves to know something intuitively when they do not really have the knowledge, and it does not seem to me to matter very much whether we express this by saying that they seemed to have intuitions but did not really, or by saying that they had intuitions but the intuitions were wrong. I have a preference, however, for the latter mode of expression because the former suggests that there is some specific recognizable psychological state, that of having intuitions, which has the proud privilege of infallibility, and this does not seem to be the case. If we say that all intuitions are true or certain, this can only be justified because we refuse to call anything an intuition if we think it false or uncertain. It is thus only verbal. We do not conclude that memory is an infallible faculty because it is bad English to say we remembered something which did not happen.

The fallibility of intuition, or if we prefer to say this, apparent intuition, enhances greatly the importance of the various testing processes to which I have referred. It seems only reasonable to regard intuition as a developing capacity and therefore capable of error, and, as we have seen, a genuine intuition may well be mixed up with false beliefs accepted on authority or derived from mistaken inference. It is not therefore a necessary condition of the validity of an intuition that everybody should agree with it. We ought to have the courage of our opinions even if everybody does not agree, and even the *certainty* of an ethical proposition is not upset by every rogue who shuts his eyes to the truth because he does not want to believe in it or every fool who cannot see it. We need not doubt that it was wrong to put Jews in concentration camps because some Nazis persuaded themselves into thinking it right. On the other hand it is even more important to insist that we must not think that what strikes us as good or right is necessarily always really so, though it is our duty to act on it as long as it really after careful consideration strikes us as so. It is not error but error which could never be corrected that would constitute a serious difficulty for the intuitionist, and there is no reason to think that ethical beliefs cannot be progressively and indefinitely improved with the help of the testing methods of which I have spoken. The uncertainty which these admissions allow must be accepted as an inevitable element in human life like all the other risks and disadvantages inherent in our limitations, but this need not prevent some ethical judgements being completely and others practically certain. Most logicians will tell you (I think quite rightly) that all the general laws which physical science establishes are, strictly speaking, uncertain, but this is not incompatible with a great many of them being practically certain, i.e. so near certainty that we need not bother about the difference, nor necessarily with some particular judgements about physical objects being absolutely certain. It is a disputed question among philosophers indeed whether any judgements at all can be absolutely certain in the strictest sense, but at least most people will be satisfied if some ethical judgements can be maintained to be at any rate as certain as the judgement, e.g. that they have bodies or that the earth existed before they were born.

An intuition must be regarded as a rational judgement, though one not based on argument, even if capable of confirmation by it, and not as a mere feeling. It is of great practical importance to realize this, for it is easy, and I should imagine common enough, to think one knows something to be true or some action right just because one has a certain kind of emotional feeling about it or even because it is the only idea which on first thoughts comes into a man's head. The best and most reliable intuition comes after reasoning and not before. There is such a thing as intuition in science, but those who excel in it are men who have already studied science carefully and systematically and practised its inferences. Intuition may even spring from reasoning in the first instance, though it goes beyond it, and it certainly must be subject to the test of reasoning. Only, since we have seen that everything we know cannot possibly be established by reasoning, we are not entitled to reject a view merely because we cannot prove it. If, though it cannot be proved, it is in accord with the rest of our well-established beliefs, and if it continues to strike us as clear and certain whenever we consider it we are entitled even in the absence of strict proof securely to hold to it.

I think, however, that intuition and inference are more closely connected than I have yet suggested. Intuition should not be regarded as a quasi-miraculous flash of insight standing by itself and not essentially linked with any other thought process at all. It presupposes at least a rational selection between different aspects of the situation, whether this is done instantaneously or gradually, and it is certainly affected deeply by our previous experience, thought and action. What I seem to see immediately when I make a particular ethical decision may be the fruit of long experience and thought about similar situations, without being itself a logical deduction or induction from definite features in the situations in question. In that case the more reasoned and reasonable my thought, the more likely is my intuition to be reliable. What presents itself as an intuition, even though it cannot be regarded as a definite inference from premises, may be determined by our whole previous slowly developed view of ethical conduct and ethical ideals. We may think of the ethical process of balancing the good and evil, the advantages and disadvantages, of one action against another as analogous to the process which occurs when we have to balance probabilities against each other in order to decide what to regard as most likely to happen or which of two theories to accept. We have to consider the points on each side, but we cannot usually thereby *prove* which act is right or which event or theory is more probable. Yet though not a matter of proof, it is a rational matter, whether we attribute the decision to "intuition" or to "good judgement," and it is certainly not one in which infallibility is general.

My insistence on intuition must not be in any way regarded as a protest against the use of reasoning in ethics. What we need is more reasoning and not less. People often talk as if modern psychology had shown that we ought not to reason: what it has shown is merely that reason does not influence us as much as we thought and that there is a lot of bad reasoning. But that reason influences us little is no ground for denying that it ought to influence us more, and that there is much bad reasoning is no ground for not trying to make it good. The deplorable effects on individual life of the neglect to use our reason properly the psychologists themselves have shown; and as regards public affairs what has happened in this generation is surely a vivid enough demonstration of the evils of irrationalism. The ideologies which have devastated the world in recent years would never have gained a grip if people had not been prepared to satisfy their emotions by accepting what was thoroughly unreasonable. The better we reason the better our intuitions: the two are not enemies but indispensable allies. It is indeed better, as is often done, to include under "reason" both reasoning and reasonable intuition. Ethics is not the same as rationality, but a reflection in particular on the extremely important virtue of justice will show the close connection between ethics and rationality. Just as the latter shows itself in logical consistency, it also shows itself in ethical consistency in the shape of applying the same principles impartially to different people. This rational impartiality and fairness is at least an essential part of moral virtue. One of the chief lines, perhaps the chief line, of moral progress through the ages has lain in making our ethics less and less inconsistent by applying the same principles more and more thoroughly to our conduct towards more and more people. The primitive man hardly recognizes any obligations at all to those outside his own tribe; the civilized man, at least in theory, recognizes obligations to the whole of humanity, if still with only very imperfect consistency in application. On the other hand it must be admitted that ethical judgements would not lead to action if they were not linked with emotion and desire. Kant refused to admit that the moral motive was a desire—he called it instead "respect for the moral law," but he had to admit that it was analogous to a desire; and it does not seem to make much difference whether we say that the motive is not a desire but admit that it is analogous to a desire, or say that it is a desire but admit, as we should have to do, that it is in important respects different from other desires.

Chapter 8

Deserts and Responsibility [1]

IN DISCUSSING ACTIONS we have so far been discussing the principles according to which we decide which action it is best to choose to do in a given situation, i.e. which action is externally the right one. But there is another way, equally ethical, of looking at actions. We look at them in this second way when we consider whether the agent deserves praise or blame, and here we think of motives rather than effects, of the inner rather than the outer side. The contrast between the two aspects of an action appears most clearly when we consider the case of a man who does something wrong in all good faith because he mistakenly thinks it right. It is apparent to every thinking person in a war where people on both sides fight with a good conscience believing that they are doing what is right, or in any case where a person acts with good intentions but makes a terrible mistake as to the consequences to be anticipated from what he does. Confronted with such cases we do not blame the agent morally for acting as he did except in so far as we think him morally responsible for his beliefs, though of course we may still blame him intellectually, i.e. call him a fool. This distinction raises some difficulties. It is a recognized principle of ethics that it is always our duty to do what after proper consideration we

---

[1] I am indebted to Messrs. Routledge and Kegan Paul for permission to use in this chapter earlier books of mine published by them.

think we ought to do, but suppose we are mistaken, then we by this principle ought to do something which is wrong and which therefore we ought not to do. Is not this a contradiction? It would be if we were not using two different senses of "ought" (and correspondingly of "right," "wrong," "duty"). Whether we are mistaken or not in our beliefs, there is clearly no morally permissible alternative to doing what we think we ought, provided we add a reservation, hard to define, about sufficient consideration. For, if we do not thus act, we cannot be acting out of moral motives but are on the contrary going against the moral principle in us, and so we ought to be blamed and not praised even if the action happens to be externally right, for that is only a matter of luck, since we did it not because it was right but thinking it wrong. Even if we accept the authority of somebody else, we do so on our own moral responsibility, and are only entitled to do so if we think him more likely to be right than ourselves. Yet the mere possibility of enquiring whether we ought to perform an action implies that there is a sense in which an action may still be wrong even if it is done with the best possible motives in the conviction that it is right. If what we thought right were automatically the right thing to do in all senses, there would be no point in devoting trouble and care to finding out what was right. We cannot answer the question what we ought to do in this other sense by pointing merely to our actual opinions and our motives. Granted that our motive is to do what is right, we still have to find out what is right. It was the nature of the principles relating to the answer to this question that I discussed in chapters 2 to 5 above, let us now turn to the question of moral blame.

Here one naturally starts by laying down the principle which I have already mentioned, namely, that we cannot be morally blamed if we do what we think right, "act in accordance with our conscience" as the phrase is. The question is not however quite so simply answered as it might seem. A man may think his conscience tells him to do the most outrageous things, as did many Nazis. Suppose Hitler believed that he was doing his duty when he inflicted appalling sufferings on the Jews and other unfortunate people and violated almost every canon of morals. Is he to escape all moral blame because he somehow deluded himself into thinking that all the abominable things he wanted to do were right or actually his duty? If he had this knack of deluding himself into believing that everything he did was right, does it follow that he was morally less blameworthy than are most people, who have a better ideal but constantly fall below it, as according to themselves have very many who would be accounted saints or almost saints? The reply would be made that Hitler was at any rate morally at fault in neglecting his duty of trying to consider properly what really was right before he acted as he did, but it is quite possible that it may not have occurred to him that he had not considered the question sufficiently, and then by the above principle he could not be blamed for neglecting that duty. But could he really escape all moral blame in this fashion? I am not therefore altogether satisfied with the above, usually accepted, principle.

But, even if we do accept it, it is important to recognize a distinction between two kinds of mistake which lead people to make wrong decisions as to what they ought to do. One kind of mistake relates to matters of fact, as when, e.g. a doctor through an error of judgement gives medicine that does harm rather than good, or a man breaks an agreement because he has genuinely misunderstood its import. Such an error is certainly not morally blameworthy unless due to negligence or avoidable prejudice, however much it may show lack of intelligence. But there is another kind of error which consists not in mistake as to matters of fact but in mistaken judgements of value. Such errors, whether morally blameworthy in the strict sense or not, at least disclose what we may call a moral defect in the person concerned. The latter is at any rate in a morally less desirable state than he would be in if he did not make such errors, whether it is "his fault" or not. An example of the first kind of error is given by a man who says something false because he thinks it true, of the second by a man who says something false because he underestimates the evil of lying or by one who attaches little value to any but "material" goods. Whether they could help it or not, it must be admitted that such men are in a lower state morally than they would be if they were free from these grave moral errors. Perhaps this is only because they are at an earlier stage of development or perhaps it is because they have knowingly done wrong in the past, but in any case they are in this state, however they got there.

For any action to have moral merit it is required not merely that it should be externally what the agent thinks right after due consideration, but that its motives should be good. What is a good and what a bad motive? There is no doubt that the desire to do one's duty because it is one's duty—I disagree with Kant in seeing no reason for not calling it a desire—is a good motive, but it is not the only one. Love for a particular person, benevolence, the desire for knowledge, the desire to create what is beautiful also can reasonably claim this title, and it is hard to refuse them it. Yet they may all lead us into evil courses on occasion if there is not at the back of our minds a moral consciousness which prevents this, so that the strictly moral motive, the desire to do what is right as such, though it need not and should not or indeed could not always be our motive, should always in a sense be present potentially. But whether a man has acted from the right motives or not on a particular occasion depends not only on the nature of the desires involved in themselves but on the context. Suppose as examiner I consciously gave a candidate a first-class mark out of love for him or out of a desire to give him pleasure (benevolence). Now love and benevolence are as such good in themselves, but I certainly could not be said to have acted from the right motives, and consequently even if he deserved such a mark my action would be morally bad, though not so bad as if I had given a third-class mark to a candidate out of the evil desire to cause him pain.[2] In either case the

---

[2] Some philosophers, however, while agreeing that actions externally right but done from bad motives are morally bad, would prefer not to call them "wrong," v. Ross, *The Right and the*

motive from which I acted ought to have had no influence at all in deciding the man's class. In other cases I might be blamed not because I acted from a motive which ought not to have influenced me at all, but because my action was not affected by other motives which ought also to have influenced me. This would be the case if I were motivated strongly by a desire for the welfare of a friend but indifferent to suffering brought on others by the way in which I sought to further that welfare. To say that a man's motive is wrong is therefore by no means necessarily to say that he is acting from a desire which is intrinsically evil. The only intrinsically evil desires are desires to produce things evil-in-themselves for their own sake, of which the most common (if not the only one) is the desire to inflict pain in anger or hatred on someone who has offended the agent. An action consciously and preventably influenced by such a desire is always blameworthy even if it be externally right, and even if it be also influenced by moral motives, as might well be the case with a person administering punishment. It is not equally clear that the desire to produce what is good in itself is always intrinsically good, for my pleasure is good in itself, yet the desire for pleasure for oneself does not seem to be intrinsically good. Reflections of this kind have suggested to some thinkers that pleasure itself is not intrinsically good in the sense in which other things are, especially moral value,[3] but this is too complicated a topic to pursue here.

So there are various ways in which even an externally right act may be blameworthy because it is wrongly motivated. On the other hand we cannot say that moral blameworthiness depends only on motives, since a man may out of a good motive do something which he believes to be wrong, e.g. steal out of love. Further, the degree of blameworthiness for a wrong act depends also on the strength of the temptation to do it: a man would be blamed much less for killing another unjustifiably if he

---

Good, pp. 4-6, and *Foundations of Ethics,* p. 114 ff., discussed in my *Definition of Good,* pp. 137-44.
[3] *v.* Ross, *Foundations of Ethics,* p. 271 ff.

did it to save his own life than if he did it to steal from the other extra beer and tobacco money, and a man is less blameworthy if owing to peculiar psychological causes a desire which would be slight in most men has become intensely strong in him. Also, other things being equal, the degree of blameworthiness will increase in proportion to the clarity with which the culprit realizes his action to be wrong. Thus, if it is a necessary condition of moral blameworthiness in the fullest sense that the agent should be conscious that he is acting wrongly, the degree of blameworthiness will increase in proportion to the clarity of this consciousness and the unsuitability of the motive, while it will decrease in proportion to the strength of the temptation.

A difficulty that has not been discussed nearly enough by philosophers is raised by what psychologists tell us about the "sub-conscious." For the latter insist that we constantly have desires of which we are not conscious, and the question is raised whether we can be blamed for these. It seems to me that in this connection it is important to bear three things in mind. (1) We cannot be morally blamed merely for the presence of a desire, whether conscious or sub-conscious, except in so far as that desire is due to previous voluntary wrong actions or abstentions from action on our part. Soldiers in the past have often thought of fear itself as shameful, but this is a mistake. There is nothing wrong about feeling fear when shells are falling all round you, cowardice consists not in being afraid but in letting fear influence our actions when they ought not to be so influenced. On the other hand the presence of a morally unsatisfactory desire such as hatred of another man imposes on us a duty to take steps towards eliminating the desire, a process which however cannot reach its goal immediately. We cannot make ourselves feel immediately quite different about someone by a mere act of will: all we can do is to will to pay attention to ideas which will gradually lessen the desire, e.g. his good points and the Christian duty of forgiveness. (2) If a desire is, strictly speaking, unconscious, i.e. if we cannot be aware of it at all, we surely cannot be blamed for not taking steps to reduce or eliminate it, however undesirable it may be, since we do not know of its existence. At least we cannot be so blamed until we have inferred it from our actions or been credibly informed of its existence by a psycho-analyst. I am not even to blame if an act which I consciously seem to myself to do out of good motives is really due to unconscious bad ones, unless the presence of the latter is again due to previous voluntary wrong acts of my own. (3) But I strongly suspect that a very great many of the so-called cases of unconscious desire are really cases where the person concerned is or has been at times conscious in some degree of the desire but without being guilty of deliberate deceit conceived as such has voluntarily turned his attention from it and refused to admit it in words even to himself. This is certainly mistaken policy, and may well be morally wrong, but, if so, in a lesser degree because his consciousness of the situation is *ex hypothesi* not very clear. People commonly do not realize the harmfulness of thus deceiving themselves or exactly what they are doing in such cases at the time they do it, and certainly a very important factor in determining the degree of guilt is the degree of the agent's awareness of the wrongness of the act. It should be noted that a person who has thus refused to take cognizance of a desire may altogether forget about it later on, indeed almost immediately, and so be quite honest when he says he has never been aware of such a desire. We need not therefore be haunted by the anxiety that in addition to any conscious guilt we may feel we are also gravely guilty because of our sub-conscious. But psycho-analysis has at least shown that deceiving oneself as to one's desires is a very dangerous practice, even if it does not carry with it much moral guilt. Certainly it seems to have been a leading cause of a great many psychological breakdowns, e.g. very many cases of "shell-shock" in the first world-war were due largely to the refusal to admit to oneself the presence of fear.

But it may be asked—are we after all to blame for anything? A negative answer to this question has sometimes been given on the ground that everything we do is determined by previous causes so that we could not have acted differently. Now I must insist at once that this "determinist" view, as it is called, though it has some considerable plausibility, is not clearly self-evident and has by no means been proved true. No proof of universal causation has as yet gained general, or indeed any considerable measure of lasting assent among philosophers. And its truth is certainly very much doubted by many contemporary scientists. As is well known, there has been a strong reaction against the belief in recent physics, though I should not like to lay much stress on this, since of such a view there cannot be either a scientific proof or a scientific disproof. Even if all events are caused, no scientist can give all their causes, and even if some are uncaused, there are no scientific means of distinguishing between the cases where there is really no cause and the cases where we merely cannot find the cause. Consequently we must regard determinism as neither proved nor disproved by arguments outside ethics, and this leaves us fully justified in rejecting it if we decide that it does really conflict with the fundamental principles of ethics. What is inconsistent with a true proposition must be rejected as false, so this mode of argument is quite legitimate. Great attention has naturally been fixed on the doubtful and disputed propositions of ethics, but in arguing for the truth of any propositions which are presupposed if there are to be any valid ethical judgements at all, the weight of the argument will be measured by those ethical judgements which are most certain. Now some ethical propositions, e.g. the proposition that I ought not to kill you, reader, because you disagree with my views, and countless others which we take for granted without questioning, are among the most certain of all propositions, and it is at least doubtful whether there is any strong case for the view that every event is completely determined by previous events. Therefore, if the latter would entail that all ethical propositions are false, or if without entailing this it would entail that all ethical propositions of the form "I (or he) ought not to do so-and-so" are false, there would be a sufficient ground for unequivocally rejecting it. For it is at any rate very much less certain than are some of the ethical propositions which it would then contradict. Now it is held that the proposition, that I ought not to do something, entails that I could avoid doing it, and that therefore I cannot be inevitably determined by previous causes to do it. This is the chief argument for what it commonly known as *free-will* or *indeterminism,* the view that whether I will or do not will to act in a certain way is something not completely determined by any previous causes.

We may grant that this indeterminist view should be accepted if it is really necessary for ethics, but is it thus necessary? Many philosophical determinists have made a case for saying that complete causal determination is not after all incompatible with the freedom indispensable for moral action, and we must at any rate start any discussion of the subject by pointing out certain ways in which people are liable to be unduly prejudiced against determinism and by showing that the effects on our ethical beliefs of the acceptance of a consistent determinist position have been exaggerated very considerably. Certainly there is a very great deal in ethics which the determinist can still retain and even defend with enthusiasm. He certainly need not and would not ordinarily deny that an act can be right in the sense of being the best act to do in the situation. The proposition that some acts are better to choose, and others worse, at least on account of their consequences, is by no means negatived by determinism. Similarly, there is nothing whatever to preclude the determinist from admitting that certain things, though determined, are intrinsically good or bad: nobody hesitates to say that pain is bad on the ground that it is caused. And he may without any inconsistency make the same judgements as to what in detail is right or wrong, intrinsically good or bad as any indeterminist (with a possible exception in the case of punishment, to which I shall refer later). He may even include among the things which are intrinsically good or bad certain acts of choice, while admitting that these acts are determined. And, as we shall see, he can give some reasonable sense even to the concepts of blame and responsibility, if not quite the full ordinary sense of the terms.

We are apt on first thoughts to regard the determinist as asserting that all our acts are determined by external causes and never by our own choice, but this is a misinterpretation of almost all philosophers of any importance who have adopted determinism. They have admitted that among the causal factors which determine whether something will happen are men's choices. They would assuredly reject the argument—Whether my child will recover from his illness or not is determined, therefore it does not matter what I do—on the ground that, although the event is determined, one of the factors which help to determine it is just the action of the child's parents. And among the factors which determine how we shall choose to act is our own character. We are apt to have an instinctive repugnance to determinism because it seems to involve saying that we are forced by something outside ourselves to act in a certain way, but the determinist may ask in reply—if it is only our own character which determines us, how is that incompatible with freedom? The character is the man, it may be said, and why should we grumble at being determined by ourselves as though we were thereby enslaved to some outside power, which would be a real interference with freedom? The determinist is of course by no means obliged to hold that all causation is physical, *prima facie* our actions are caused by desires and choices or acts of will. Am I not free if I do what I want, and therefore choose, to do?

Nor is determinism incompatible with change and improvement of character, even in the extreme form it sometimes takes in "conversion." "Character" normally stands for the habits according to which a man usually acts, and these of course may change very considerably. What the determinist will say is that, apart from the influence of external circumstances, which cannot settle everything, such changes are always due to something more fundamental in the nature of the man. All bad men would not be converted by the influence that converts any one particular man; for him to be so affected he must be the sort of man who would first go through a course of "sowing his wild oats" and then, when he came under a certain influence, change violently. If so, that was part of his character in a wider sense. Even inanimate substances may change in such a way that they have in a sense quite a different character at one time from what they have at another, e.g. molten iron not only looks very different but acts very differently from iron in a solid state, but this change of character does not mean that the melting of iron is not determined by causes. It follows from the fundamental nature of iron that it will behave in one way in the solid and in quite another in the molten state.

It must be added that we are constantly in our practical actions presupposing that there are psychological as well as physical causes at work affecting human volition. If there were not, we could not make the assumptions about their results on which most of our actions depend. It would be pointless, for instance, even to go into a shop to buy something if we did not assume that the desire to earn money had some effect on the wills of men. All that the indeterminist can possibly maintain is that volitions are not *completely* determined, though they are always influenced by causation and can often be predicted with a probability that approximates to certainty from our knowledge of the man concerned and of the laws of psychological causation. But this is also all he need maintain. He may admit that a man has motives for sinning which depend on external causes and on his psychological temperament. He may also admit that the sin is rendered much more likely and much more difficult to avoid by, e.g. the man's upbringing or his yielding to previous temptations, but he will remain an indeterminist as long as he refuses to admit that these circumstances make the sin inevitable. Even if it is likely, as long as it is not inevitable, he will say, it can still be a sin. Nor need the indeterminist hold that anything but our volitions is not completely determined by causes. All other aspects of our mental life may be completely subject to them. He must even admit, if he is to give an intelligible account of his views, that free acts of will are caused by the agent. I certainly should not be responsible for my acts if I had not caused them: they would not indeed be my acts. All he can maintain intelligibly is that my free acts, though caused by me in some way, are such that their nature is not fixed either by things or events external to myself or by events in my previous history or even by my own previous character, or by all these factors together, i.e. not fixed by the past.

It is sometimes thought to be an adequate refutation of determinism to point out that we can act against "the strongest desire." For it is assumed that on the determinist view our actions are determined by our desires and that therefore the strongest desire will always win. I think, however, that indeterminists who say this, as well as many determinists, are misled by an ambiguity in "strongest desire." This phrase may mean "the desire which prevails," and in that case of course we cannot act against it, but this is merely to say that we never act against the desire in accordance with which we do act, a statement which is indeed true but not of the least interest. But it may mean—and this is the interesting sense—the desire which we feel most strongly. Now there is no contradiction whatever in supposing that a man's actions might be always completely determined by some causes or other, and yet that they are not always determined by the desire which he feels most strongly. If there is a law according to which a man's actions are necessarily determined by the strongest desire in this sense, it is a causal law, and whether a causal law holds is a matter to be settled not by logic but by an appeal to experience. Determinism is the view that all human acts are caused, not that they are caused in any particular fashion. Even if we assume that all action is caused by some desire, we have no reason for assuming that the causal efficacy of a desire is always in proportion to its felt strength. There is no evidence whatever in favour of this view, and the empirical evidence is dead against it. There is an empirical fact such a thing as moral struggle and the overcoming of temptation, where a man resists a desire to which it would be easier to yield, but its occurrence does not necessarily prove determinism false. That a deliberate effort of will sometimes prevents the desire felt most strongly from leading to action is just another fact about the causes of action. Indeed I should have thought one was liable to feel a desire most strongly just when one had decided to act against it. For, other things being equal, one would expect to feel a desire most keenly towards that which one has been immediately before cut off from having, especially when the deprivation is due to one's own voluntary action, though one's desires would soon tend to readjust themselves in the less acute cases of conflict.

But surely after all we could not be responsible or to blame if we could not have acted differently? The determinist may admit even this, only analysing the meaning of "could" differently from the indeterminist. Obviously even a determinist must recognize a distinction between the case where a man does something voluntarily and the case where he does it because his arm is pushed. In the latter case his desires and volitions are irrelevant, in the former case he only does it because he desires and so chooses or wills to do it (or at least does not will to restrain his desire to do it). Thus "could" has been defined on the determinist view as meaning "would if the agent had chosen." Now there is certainly no point in blaming a man if he could not have acted differently in this sense of "could." For the point of blame is to induce the man blamed to decide, or at least to try harder, to act differently on future occasions, but it will not achieve this object in cases where the man's volitions do not affect what happens. But blame may be effective without presupposing that the man could have acted differently everything else being what it was (the indeterminist sense of "could"), provided only he has a desire to avoid acts which he considers blameworthy or at least knows to be blamed in fact (though the latter is of course a less worthy reason). And the same applies to punishment. A way of preventing people from doing wrong in the future is to make things unpleasant for them on account of the wrong they have done in the past, and since no determinist would deny that pain or the risk of pain is liable to cause changes in people's volitions, this may be effective both on the determinist and on the indeterminist view. The indeterminist would however say that this only shows that punishment can still be expedient if determinism is true, not that it can be just or deserved. For the latter condition to be fulfilled, he will contend, the culprit must have acted wrongly of his own free will in the sense that no causes determined him so to act. Of this I shall say more later.[4] However, the determinist can give a good reason for not applying blame and punishment to involuntary defects such as unavoidable ill-health or ignorance on the ground that these do not depend on any defects of will and therefore on anything that could be cured by blame or punishment. There is thus a morally important and intelligible sense of "could" in which a man could have acted differently even on the determinist theory, and this sense at least is undoubtedly presupposed by blame. The issue between determinist and indeterminist is not whether men could have acted differently from the way in which they did act, but what the sense of "could" is in which they could have acted differently. The indeterminist holds that a man could have acted differently, everything else including his previous character being the same: the determinist denies this and means by "could have acted differently" that he could have done so except for certain circumstances internal to himself. We might call it the distinction between the absolute and the relative sense of "could."

Blame perhaps usually is but need not be a purely utilitarian concept for the determinist. He may admit that a bad will, or unwillingness to obey one's conscience, is intrinsically evil and not merely harmful in its effects, and he may define moral blame as the assertion that some act is due to badness of will. Blame of a wicked act will be then appropriate in itself as well as possibly having good effects. It will be equivalent, where justified, to saying that something is bad which is really bad in itself. He can thus retain a considerable part of the common-sense

---

[4] v. below p. 143 ff.

conception of moral responsibility and blameworthiness. But he cannot retain the whole of it. For the conception of common-sense ethics involves the idea that a free action might have been different the agent being what he was. This the determinist cannot admit: he can only admit that the action might have been different, the circumstances external to the agent's character being what they were, and that does not seem enough.

The indeterminist, on the other hand, will contend that, while some intrinsic goods and evils may be determined, an action can never have the quality of *moral* goodness or *moral* badness if determined. He will insist that the sense we have of remorse and shame for an act just derives its sting from a realization of the fact that we could have acted differently, whatever our previous actions and states of mind may have been. It is all very well to say that on the determinist view what determines us is our own previous character and past acts, but if we are determined by the past, it is replied, we are not free *now,* for we are not *now* able to change the past acts on which our present acts depend. And the same would apply to any past time at which any of the acts which determined us now were performed, for they would be determined by a still earlier past. Worse still, it is said by the determinist that what we do is always determined by our character together with our circumstances, but how was our character acquired? In so far as it was determined by our circumstances, we were admittedly not free; in so far as it was inherited, surely it was not we but our ancestors (if anybody) who were responsible for it? And the same would apply to them and so on till we got back to the first man or to God. Whenever we began to exist, our existence and original nature must on the determinist view have been produced by some causes; and since we did not exist before we came into existence, these causes cannot lie in us. Hence the determinist cannot effectively defend himself by saying that he is only asserting determination by oneself, for in the long run this turns into determination by someone or something other than oneself.

The determinist who is in earnest with ethics will have

to say in reply that it remains true that a man's will is bad now, however he acquired it, and that this is, or ought to be, the meaning of blame. Moral blame will still differ from a mere deploring of what is unsatisfactory, like the weather or the incurable stupidity of a congenital idiot, because it has reference to a bad will and therefore to a different, though still determined, kind of badness. A bad disposition of will is still bad, even if its possessor just inherited it, and it is therefore still rational to condemn it. Further, it is an essential part of the man in a way in which his misfortunes or bad physical health are not, and therefore in condemning it we are condemning the man, saying he is fundamentally bad. But the determinist will stress mainly the social utility of blame and punishment.

Most readers will, I have no doubt, feel after considering the above account that determinism does not do full justice to the conception of responsibility, as we cannot or can hardly help holding it in our ordinary life. When we blame other people or ourselves, we do really think in an indeterminist and not a determinist way. But is this an adequate refutation of the determinist? It is not as if, like, e.g. in my opinion subjectivist or naturalist theories, determinism contradicted the very foundations of our ethical thought. We could then argue that this theory would make all ethical judgements false, and that many ethical judgements are much more certain than determinism could be even on the most favourable view. But we have seen that the determinist can give an account which does much more justice to ethics and even to moral responsibility than appeared possible at first sight. It is not the whole of ethics which is at stake between the determinist and the indeterminist, but the relatively subordinate, though very important, concept of moral responsibility, and even here the determinist may argue plausibly that he can leave a place for most of what the plain man means by this, indeed it would be said by some, all of what he means that is really intelligible. All divergencies from what strikes one as common-sense ethics are clearly not to be ruled out on principle, if only because there is no such thing as "the common-sense view," there being a marked difference between the common-sense views of different times and civilizations. And that being so, how much we are to accept becomes a difficult question of degree, though we can be quite sure about some divergencies that they are so large as to be intolerable. Considerable weight must be attached to such widespread and convincing ethical beliefs as those which imply indeterminism, common as I suppose they are to all cultures, except where these have been influenced by explicit philosophical or theological arguments to the contrary, especially if the philosopher himself finds that he cannot get rid of them in his normal thinking about ethical matters, but some degree of confusion and divergence from the real truth is even then not necessarily excluded. We might therefore be entitled to revise our common-sense view of responsibility if there were a really strong case for determinism on its own metaphysical merits, but it may be doubted whether such a case has been presented. Our ability to predict human actions can be quite adequately explained by admitting the occurrence of causes which incline us to certain actions, so that these are usually performed, but do not make them inevitable. After all, whether determinism or indeterminism is true, we cannot predict with certainty and do not know all the causes.

We have omitted here a consideration of various theories which have been put forward by way of compromise or to gain the advantages of both sides. They agree with ordinary determinism in maintaining that all acts are caused but try to avoid its difficulties by refining on the concept of mental causation. They are very difficult, and it is impossible to go into them without delving into metaphysics. All I shall say here is that, while they go some way towards bridging the gulf, they still leave open the fundamental antithesis between those who hold that our nature being what it is we could still have acted differently and those who take the opposite view.

It is to be feared that the acceptance of determinism might lead to a deterioration of the sense of moral responsibility and the finding of excuses for neglecting one's duty. It is therefore very important to be clear as to the fallaciousness of arguments such as that, if everything is determined, it does not matter what we do. That determinism will *necessarily* lead to such a weakening of moral fibre is disproved by the example of people like the Puritans whose well-known moral enthusiasm and moral strictness were combined with a strong belief in determinism. On the other hand the determinist way of approach in recent times (though not, I am afraid, with the earlier Puritans) has made for greater tolerance and a more humane treatment of wrongdoers. Psychological explanations have been given which at least make their actions less inexcusable, if they do not make them inevitable, and it is pointed out that they are often the victims of social evils not under their control. Practically it is perhaps a good dictum for most purposes that we should adopt the indeterminist attitude towards ourselves and the determinist attitude towards other men, in the sense that we should think of ourselves as capable of going against all the causes by which the psychologist would explain our conduct but be prepared always to look for the causes to explain the unsatisfactory conduct of other men. Even if he has some undetermined free will, we never know how much or how little the other man is to blame, and it is not our business (except where necessary in certain respects for practical purposes) to be his judge. Yet we must not of course carry out this maxim without qualification. It is the dictator or unscrupulous politician who takes a thoroughly determinist view of others to be moulded as means for his ends, and we may be unduly discouraged or else attempt the impracticable if we take no account of the limitations imposed on us by our present character and past life.

In any case we must not think of the alternatives for a man as just being absolutely free apart from physical limitations and having no freedom at all: freedom is very much a matter of degree, whether we think of it as consisting in independence of causes other than our own preference or in independence of causes altogether. Even if some acts are undetermined, they are inevitably at least conditioned and limited by many causes, and even if they are primarily the result of our preferences causes external to the man play a large part in thus determining and limiting him. Philosophers and moralists have frequently insisted that in a very important sense the good man is more free than the bad. This is most plainly the case where we are thinking of the badness of the weak-willed man who yields to almost every strong impulse as it arises. For the way in which one exercises one's freedom of choice at a particular time may gravely limit one's freedom at other times, and a man cannot be said to be very free now if by misuse of his freedom on earlier occasions he has made it physically or psychologically impossible to attain what he desires. A habitual drunkard or a man who flies into violent passions in which he gives grave offence to others may put limitations on his own future actions greater and more irksome than those imposed by most dictators on most of their subjects. If we take the case of the morally bad but self-controlled man, who pursues wicked or selfish ends with prudence and cool resoluteness, it does not seem however by any means so clear that he loses in freedom when we compare him with the equally prudent and resolute good man, and it may even seem as if the latter shackles himself by his scruples and considerateness for other men. But it may be argued that what even the bad man wants is full satisfaction and that, since this goal cannot from the nature of the case be reached by the road he follows, he will never, as long as he remains bad, be free to fulfil his desires. For though, as I insisted earlier,[5] the happiness of a man is by no means necessarily in proportion to his goodness, it remains true that there is a certain fulness of satisfaction which can only be obtained by the good man, and which we may expect that the bad man also would want above everything if he knew what it was really like. We certainly must not therefore say that the bad man has no freedom —if so, he would not be responsible for his wrong actions,

---

[5] *v.* above p. 24 ff.

since responsibility requires freedom either in the indeterminist or at least in the determinist sense—only that he has less freedom than the good.[6]

Linked with the question of freedom but still a quite different one is that of punishment. This subject is best discussed in terms of two sharply conflicting theories. According to one, generally known as the retributive theory, it is an end in itself that a man should suffer pain in proportion to his deserts and this is the primary and main purpose of punishment, though of course it may also have socially useful results and even help to reform the individual punished. According to the other, the utilitarian theory, punishment is justified only by its consequences and is always undesirable in itself. The former theory is certainly more natural to mankind: most people strongly tend to think that it is intrinsically fitting that a man should "get his deserts." If we hear for instance of a monstrous case of cruelty, most of us have a strong feeling that it is very inappropriate not only on account of its effects but in itself that a man who does such things should go on enjoying himself (even in other, not immoral ways) and should not suffer for his wickedness. That wrongdoers ought to be punished irrespective of any advantage to be gained for themselves or others from their punishment seems to have been a most widespread and influential belief from very early days. It is, however, a belief about which reflection raises grave doubts and which has been subjected to severe attacks by many thinkers in recent times.

The retributive theory has a special connection with indeterminism in that almost everybody who holds it probably considers, if he reflects, that punishment can only be just if the man punished could have acted differently, his character and circumstances still being what they were. I do not see indeed that a determinist would contradict himself if he maintained the theory, but I have never heard of one who did so. On the other hand the retributive theory of punishment seems to me itself to be

---

[6] For my views on freedom v. also *The Fundamental Questions of Philosophy,* chap. IX (Routledge and Kegan Paul, 1951).

in too shaky a position to provide a safe argument for indeterminism.

It is certainly plain at any rate that the retributive theory cannot stand as a complete account of the function of punishment. Even if it is good-in-itself that people should suffer in proportion to the wrong they have done, it is certainly not the only good. Now there could hardly be a guarantee that the treatment most in accord with a malefactor's deserts would also always be that most conducive to the general good, and in a case where it is not, the advantage of punishing retributively would have to be set against the other goods lost or the evil inflicted by doing so. Consequently retribution cannot possibly be the only function of punishment: utilitarian considerations must also have a place in determining whether a guilty man should be punished and the amount of the punishment. And once we start balancing the good of retribution in itself and the other goods involved against each other, the latter appear so much more important that it looks as if the good of retribution, for whatever it is worth, would have to be sacrificed to them in almost every case where there was a conflict, thus giving us an almost purely utilitarian theory in practice. It is obvious that, even if it is desirable in itself that a man should be retributively punished, it is much more desirable that he should be reformed and other people deterred from crime, and therefore the first good, if it is a good, should be sacrificed to the others, at least except in cases where there is only a very slight detriment to the latter.

But criticism can go further than this. On reflection grave doubts are raised not only as to whether retribution is the main function of punishment but as to whether it is a legitimate function at all, thus leading to the conclusion that the sole and not only the chief justification of punishment lies in its effects. Firstly, there seems to be a highly suspicious connection between belief in retributive punishment and a strong native tendency in men which is certainly very far from being morally commendable, anger and the desire for revenge. It cannot be denied that it is natural to want to hurt somebody who has wrongly hurt oneself, but all advanced ethical and religious systems have strongly fought against this tendency. The reader need not be informed that to yield to it is directly in conflict, for instance, with the teaching of Christianity, which preaches instead the duty of forgiving one's enemies. The advocate of the retributive theory will reply by drawing a sharp distinction between the desire for revenge and the sense of justice which, he holds, requires that men should suffer pain in proportion to their misdeeds, and he will support the distinction by pointing out that we feel the appropriateness of punishment not only in cases where the wrongdoer has injured us, but in cases where he has done something which does not in the least affect our interests personally but only those of strangers to us. Further, a man may feel it even when the wrongdoer is himself. People have often been strongly convinced that they ought to "atone" for their own sins by suffering, and have sometimes actually asked to be punished themselves. Even if they do not go so far as this, surely most people do have a somewhat different feeling about those of their misfortunes which they regard as brought on them by their own fault and those which seem to them accidental. This answer is not conclusive: it may be the case that the desire for revenge first caused the idea that retribution was good in regard to acts done against oneself and one's family, and that the influence of this idea was then extended by sympathy to cover cases where the victim of wrong was a stranger, and even by a process of generalized reasoning to cover oneself. Once the idea that retributive punishment was in general right had been formed under the influence of this motive, men would be forced by logic to apply the theory to themselves if they reasoned consistently, and people do sometimes reason consistently. But, while this explanation may be correct, I do not see how it can be at all conclusively established, and must therefore admit that the argument does not demolish the retributive theory. Such considerations do however make clear the great danger of revengeful and sadistic tendencies finding vent under the unconscious disguise of a righteous indignation calling for just punishment, since the evil desire for revenge, if not identical with the latter, bears a resemblance to it sufficiently close to deceive those who want an excuse. Of this a most melancholy illustration is provided by the history of the penal systems of the past.

As regards the duty of forgiveness it has been said that the person whose business it is to inflict punishment for a wrong act and the person whose duty it is to forgive it are not usually the same person, at least in a civilized community (though they undeniably sometimes are, in the case of offences which are not punished by law, but by some form of social or economic pressure). It is not the business of the private citizen as such, still less of the man wronged, legally to punish a crime, though it may be his duty to take steps that somebody else may punish it. But whether the offender is to be punished or not and how much, is normally decided by people unaffected personally by the offence, and it is not necessarily a virtue in them to forgive the offender. The point of forgiveness lies in the man who was wronged being himself the man who forgives. Other people have not anything to forgive. And it is just because the man who would be expected to find it hardest to do so goes out of his way to return good for evil that forgiveness sometimes has a specially shaming and redeeming effect on the sinner. But forgiveness need not always consist in enabling the person forgiven to escape a deserved punishment, even where this is possible, and when it does so it might be regarded as in a similar position to other acts which involve the breaking of a general rule in the interests of the greater good. To admit that an offender should sometimes be pardoned is not incompatible with saying that punishment is an end-in-itself, because what is itself good may be sacrificed for the sake of other goods. It may, however, be questioned whether we do or should feel like this about forgiveness. If the culprit can be forgiven in a way which involves no infliction of punishment and this produces the best result, is anything lost? Is it not really sheer gain, whereas on the retributive theory it should involve the loss of one good-in-itself, deserved punishment?

It is further objected that pain in itself is an evil and

that therefore it must be wrong to inflict it except for a future good which outweighs the evil. Even if the sin for which pain is inflicted is evil in itself, how can one evil be made less by adding a second? No doubt the pain may help to prevent a repetition of the sin, but to say this is to justify the punishment by reference to its effects and not as an end in itself. The retributionist may reply that, whether a thing is evil depends not only on its own quality but on its context and relations, and here what is relevant is not just the fact that the punishment is painful but the fact that he pain is inflicted for doing wrong. But it seems very odd indeed that what is in any other context the most abominable of acts, namely, the deliberate infliction of pain on somebody else for pain's sake, should be made right and even a duty just because the man concerned has previously done wrong. It is all very well to talk about atoning for one's sins, but no amount of atonement can wipe out the past act. Further, it is fitting to rejoice in what is good in itself, therefore if it is an end-in-itself that the guilty should suffer, it is fitting to rejoice in their sufferings. But surely that is not the case: it is not fitting to gloat over the pain of anyone, even if he is a thoroughly bad man.

Finally it may be doubted whether there is any sense in talking of a correspondence between such incommensurables as suffering and moral badness. And, even if there is, it is quite impracticable for us to try to establish such a correspondence in practice. The State can punish people for specific offences, but it cannot possibly estimate the moral character of offenders as a whole and the happiness they would enjoy if unpunished, and diminish the latter to just such an extent that happiness and character are in proportion. Still less could it do this for all members of the community, and if not, can it be retributively just to pounce with severe punishments on a small section of the population, who are by no means necessarily all worse than all the respectable persons out of prison, to say nothing of the suffering indirectly inflicted on innocent relatives? The penal system may be justified by expediency, but it certainly cannot be justified as a move towards establishing a due retributive proportion between badness and suffering. The latter, if it be an end at all, is an end for God not for man, and any attempt to further it by man is likely either to produce as much retributive injustice as justice or to involve intolerable interference with individual liberty or both. It is much better to adopt the principle of giving as much happiness to others as we can without bothering whether they deserve it by their moral goodness except in cases where to do so produces clear harm.

A utilitarian theory of punishment, on the other hand, which incidentally need not commit us to utilitarianism in any form as a general theory of ethics, will base itself on two main kinds of effect. In the first place it will insist on the deterrent tendency of punishment, by which is commonly meant its tendency to make people other than the man punished afraid to commit similar offences. And, secondly, it will point to the reformatory effects of punishment, i.e. the effect punishment is hoped to have in the way of the improvement of the man punished himself. Here we have a rational justification of punishment which only appeals to what is by general admission good. For everyone will agree that it is desirable that criminals should be reformed and that people should be induced not to commit crimes. Careful investigation has undoubtedly disclosed great limitations in the capacity of punishment to achieve these ends, but no one can deny that there are cases in which it does contribute to them. Only an unreasonable fanatic could say that punishment by the State has no effect in deterring possible criminals and that crime would not enormously increase without it; and grossly exaggerated as its value has no doubt been in the past I do not see how one can maintain that punishment in at least its milder forms has no place at all in the education of children. I am more sceptical about the utility of punishment as such in reforming criminals (for, though imprisonment does provide an opportunity for other reformatory influences to be brought to bear on the prisoner, this must be regarded as reformation while being punished rather than reformation by the punishment as such); and in the case of punishment in education we are usually not much concerned with the deterrence of children other than the one actually punished. But this still leaves plenty of scope for deterrence by State punishment and the use of reformatory punishment in education, though the latter should as far as possible take the forms of letting the offence have its natural consequences (where these are not too bad) and of verbal blame.

It is, however, harder than is often thought to shed all retributive elements in one's theory of punishment. Suppose that in a particular case it is impossible to find the real criminal, but suppose also that we have got hold of a person generally believed guilty so that the deterrent effects of punishing him would be the same as if he really were guilty. Suppose, further, that psychological experts could assure us that his character would benefit by a spell of imprisonment. (Even a very good man's character often benefits by suffering: very possibly it is more likely than a bad man's to do so.) That surely would not make the punishment right, yet it ought to on the utilitarian theory. The latter theory does not give an adequate account of one of our strongest moral convictions, namely, that it is atrociously bad to punish innocent persons for the sake of utility. Doubts have been raised earlier as to whether there are any general laws which could under no circumstances be broken, but the principle that we ought not gravely to punish innocent people comes about as near to being such a law as any general law about our acts can do. And, in general, the utilitarian theory, as usually stated at least, seems to overlook the point that punishment has an essential reference to the past and that justice does not consist merely in producing good consequences. We always punish people for something already done, and to say a punishment is useful is not the same as to say it is just, even if in general just punishments are useful. These considerations suggest a view according to which the retributive theory is brought in to decide whether we have the right to punish a man at all and the utilitarian theory to decide whether we are to exercise this right and how much punishment, if any, we are to inflict. It seems that only wrongdoing against a pre-existing law can give a State the right to punish but that whether this right is exercised or not should be decided by utilitarian considerations, except that it offends against justice not only to punish the innocent but to punish those guilty of lesser offences more heavily than those guilty of greater.

Secondly, suppose two worlds in which there was the same amount of happiness and unhappiness, but in one of which the bad were happy and the good unhappy, and in the other the bad were unhappy and the good happy. It seems plain that the latter world would be preferable to the former. Many would go further and say that it is less bad that a thoroughly wicked man should be unhappy than that he should be happy, even if the results were the same and there were no hope of curing him of his wickedness, but this is a rather more dubious proposition. In any case it is not our business to try to establish a proportion between happiness and goodness, unhappiness and badness, even if that be desirable in the abstract.

It seems to me that the most illuminating fashion in which I can look at punishment is to think of it as a more emphatic way of telling a man that he has done wrong. How can punishment possibly reform a man? Fear of a repetition of the pain indeed might cause him not to repeat the offence, but only out of quite non-moral motives, and on this ground some people have altogether condemned punishment. It may be legitimately replied that it is at any rate a less unsatisfactory situation if a man abstains from crimes out of non-moral motives than if he commits them out of equally non-moral motives, and perhaps even that what he first avoids out of bad motives he will often later avoid out of good, but this is not the only rejoinder to be made. Punishment is not merely the infliction of pain but the infliction of pain for previous wrongdoing. Now why will people do what is wrong? Some do so because they believe it right or even their duty, and I do not see how punishment is likely to reform these; but except for political offenders the great majority of people in prison are there for doing what they know to be wrong. But if a man does what he knows to be wrong, this is because he is not sufficiently vividly conscious of the wrongness to stop him from doing it when swayed by a more or less strong desire, and the problem of the reformer is to increase the vividness of this realization. This may be done by pointing out the wrongness of the act to him in words, but a more emphatic method of impressing it on the offender is often needed for criminals and even for naughty children, hence punishment. Of course the fact that it is punished does not prove an action to be wrong, but what is wanted to reform the man is not that he should know his acts to be wrong, which he already does, but that he should realize more vividly that they are wrong, and to be punished for them may well increase the vividness of this realization. Punishment, whether it takes the severer form of imprisonment or the milder form of being put on probation, is more impressive and more difficult to forget than merely verbal blame. This way of looking at punishment explains the reference to a past wrong act on which the retributive theory dwells. Punishment can only reform if it can be viewed by the offender as an appropriate expression of disapproval for an act which he really did and which was really wrong, and indeed it also often owes a great deal of its deterrent effect to being an expression of disapproval, i.e. a "disgrace." It seems to me, however, very important to realize that the pain of punishment is always itself an evil, to be avoided where possible, not as on the retributive theory a good. And if in any particular case the infliction of additional pain, beyond any mental pain which may be inevitably involved in the offender's repentant realization that he has done wrong, can be avoided, punishment is not there the fitting expression of disapproval and thus loses any value it may have.

While punishment thus can have some value, it is of more practical importance to stress its limitations, since there are factors in human nature which strongly tend to its excessive use. Punishment is the simplest method of reaction to offences and one strongly supported by the natural instinct to hit back, it is therefore the first refuge of the mentally lazy, whereas it should be almost the last. And the extent to which a system of punishments is liable to abuse and the psychological damage it may cause are well enough known to-day. The word "punishment" may be used in an extended sense to cover all sorts of blame and therefore every way of teaching a person that he has done something which he had better not have done, but understood as the deliberate infliction of pain, bodily or mental, other than what comes naturally from the sense of having done wrong, it should be regarded as of decidedly minor importance as an agency of reform.[7]

* * *

There are at least two respects in which this book may be deemed very inadequate. Firstly, it may be objected that I have not done justice to the close connection between the individual and society and so said far too little about social ethics or social philosophy. To this the reply is that it is not relevant to the truth or falsity of a man's ethical ideas whether or how he in fact derived them from society. It is not the history of the development of ethical ideas that we are discussing but their validity, which may be quite independent of the authority on which we originally accepted them. As for the application of ethics to social and political organizations, this is a separate subject of study normally distinguished from Ethics as such and called Political or Social Philosophy, so that it does not usually form a part of books on Ethics. I certainly have not space to incorporate a discussion of it in my book, but I should insist that the general ethical principles I have laid down here apply equally to the conduct of governments towards their people and towards other States in so far as the situation is parallel to any in which they can be applied to the individual.

Secondly, it may be objected that I have not given the reader much definite practical advice as to what he ought to do even as an individual. On this point I must refer critics to what I said in the first chapter.[8] The decision

---

[7] For a full account of my views on this question *v.* my book *The Morality of Punishment* (Routledge and Kegan Paul, 1929).

[8] *v.* above p. 16 ff.

what we ought to do in a given situation depends on knowledge of various kinds of which only part is ethical, and even that part depends more on an intuitive insight into the values relevant to the particular situation or, if you prefer the phrase, a good common-sense judgement of these, than on anything which could be established by philosophical argument, while for the other part we shall have to obtain our information from natural science or from the common-sense knowledge of the world and of other people which with everyday practical problems not calling for specialists can often take the place of science. It is because a good philosopher need by no means be equally good in realizing and utilizing this knowledge or possess the kind of practical insight requred that it is not true, as Plato held it was, that philosophers ought to rule the State, but we may still hold that those who do rule States would be better for a training in philosophic Ethics and wish they had more of the impartiality, broad-mindedness and objectivity which go with the philosophic spirit. If they had had all only even a very minor degree of this we should have been spared the horrors of Nazi and Communist fanaticism as well as many less gross evils. Philosophical Ethics may and should still have an important indirect influence on ordinary practical ethics.

In another respect what the philosopher can do to promote ethical conduct is still more limited. Even if he can tell us how we ought to act, I fully realize that the major part of the ethical task is to bring ourselves to do what we believe we ought to do: it is far easier to form good ideals than to live up to the ideals we have formed, and to persuade a person by reasoning that something is his duty is by no means necessarily to induce him to do it. That is the work of the preacher, the practical psychologist and the candid and sympathetic friend, not of the philosopher *qua* philosopher.

Note to Chapter 6

There is one naturalist view of good, discussion of which I omitted in the first edition, but which has become prominent in thought lately.[1] According to this view the objective meaning of "good" is just equated with a list of the kinds of things which actually are good. This I should criticize on the following grounds.
(*a*) They surely have something in common in respect of which they are all called good. In fact, if they are good in themselves, they must have at least this in common that they are for their own sake right objects of pursuit or at least of some favourable attitude. Further, I think it is plain that nothing which is not good in itself could have this property. Consequently, if there is no other common property peculiar to them, it would be reasonable to make this the definition of "good in itself." This would not be a naturalist definition unless right were itself analysed naturalistically. I have not argued against all definitions of good but only against a definition of good in terms which are not specifically ethical.
(*b*) If to say that a certain kind of thing is good just means that it belongs to a certain wider class, this does not tell one anything unless something more is being said than is said by merely listing the subspecies of the class in question. For instance, "happiness is good" would be a purely verbal proposition if it meant no more than that happiness belongs to the class comprising e.g. happiness, love, knowledge, beauty, this class being defined merely by giving a list of its sub-classes.
(*c*) Even if such a definition of good could be defended as adequate, this would not show that ought or right could be defined naturalistically. It is surely completely plain that "I ought to do this" does not just *mean*: this hurts people unnecessarily or this involves breaking a promise, etc. The view also seems liable to the objections I brought against all naturalist theories except that what I said on page 92 perhaps cannot be applied to it.

Note to Chapter 7

In this chapter I did not lay enough stress on a compromise view which has become prominent recently, though I did mention it.[2]

---

[1] *v.* Hare, *The Language of Morals;* Nowell-Smith, *Ethics.* Since these writers hold that the main function of ethical "judgements" is to commend and not to state, their views as a whole, however, fall rather under the next chapter.
[2] p. 119, *v.* Toulmin, *Reason in Ethics,* ch. 2-3; Barnes in *Proceedings of Aristotelian Soc.,* Supp. Vol. XXII, p. 1ff.; Macdonald in *Philosophical Analysis,* ed. M. Black, p. 211ff.

According to this view "ethical judgements" are not properly described as true or false because they are too unlike scientific judgements, but they can still be valid or invalid, rational or irrational. This view would escape the strongest objections to subjectivism, provided the judgement that an "ethical judgement" is "valid" is not itself analysed naturalistically or subjectively. For the view admits that there can be good reasons and not merely persuasive arguments for taking some ethical attitudes rather than others. It, like Moore's view, safeguards the unique character of ethics, insisting that "ethical judgements" have their own proper criteria of validity which need not be reduced to the criteria of natural science. At the same time it insists on the point that to say that something is good or bad is not like adding another factual quality to its description. A person who holds this view need not try to answer the question what "ethical judgements" are by giving a simple watertight definition. He need not say they are commands or decisions or statements or emotional expressions. He may insist that they constitute a unique class which has analogies with all these kinds of expressions but cannot be reduced to any one of them, and that as such they have reasons of their own to justify them which are as valid in their own sphere as the reasons of science are in hers, reasons which will not indeed prove anything logically or scientifically but will provide an adequate justification for a mental attitude or an action.

I have much more sympathy with this view than I have with the outright subjectivism which I discussed in Chapter 7 or with naturalism. But I still think that those who put it forward have erred in limiting truth to propositions capable of empirical or scientific establishment. If we are to go by ordinary usage, the word is commonly employed also in such disputable fields as theology, and its meaning seems to lie in what we are aiming at when we judge and not in the kind of criteria which lead us to call a proposition true. To limit truth by definition so as to coincide with scientific truth is to assume without proof that the only reality is that discoverable by natural science; to limit it to cases where there are agreed criteria is to admit only truths which can be discovered with relative ease and assurance. It has been argued that it is not the natural linguistic usage to apply "true" or "false" to "ethical judgements" as it is with ordinary judgements, but it is certainly not linguistically incorrect or very unusual. Further, the terms "know" and "believe" are constantly used in connection with ethical judgements, but if a judgement asserts something which can be known or believed it can be true. It certainly is arguable that ethical judgements are not true in precisely the same sense of "true" as are the judgements of natural science, but the same might be said of the judgements of immediate experience or the judgements of mathematics. There may still be a more general sense of truth in which they are all true.

Bibliography

Plato: Republic, Bks. 1-4

Aristotle: Nicomachean Ethics, Bks. 1-7, 10

Mill: Utilitarianism

Kant: Groundwork of the Metaphysic of Morals, Trl. Paton

Moore: Principia Ethica, and Ethics

Field: Moral Theory

Carritt: The Theory of Morals

Ross: The Right and the Good

Hare: The Language of Morals

Index

Approval, definitions of ethical concepts in terms of, 82-84, 108-109
A Priori, and empirical knowledge, 52 ff.
Arguments in ethics, 105-106, 108, 116 ff., 124 ff., 157
Aristotle, 31
Ayer (A. J.), 102 n.

Barnes (W.), 156 n.
Bentham, 23
Biological definitions of ethical terms, 88-89
Blame, 63, 126-132, 139 ff.
Broad (C. D.), 90 n., 97

Categorical, hypothetical imperatives, 50-51
Certainty in ethics, 122-123
Christianity, 34, 59, 146
Common-sense ethics, 9-11, 26-27, 75, 98, 141-142
Consequences, in ethics, 52-53, 56-59, Chap. 5 passim, 113, 121

Definitions, 17-19, Chap. 6 passim
Desires, 29-30, 51-52, 80-81, 85-88, 92, 125-126, 129-132, 137-138
Determinism, 133-136
Dewey (J.), 13
Differences of view in ethics, 111-118
Duty, 15, 50 ff. *v.* Ought

Egoism, Chap. 2 passim
Emotive function of "ethical judgements" 104 ff.
End, means, 12-15, 59, 69 ff.
Errors, moral, 126-129
Ethics, nature of, Chap. 1 passim
Evil, intrinsic, 130
Evolution, 88-89

Field (G. C.), 87 n.
Forgiveness, 148
Freedom, 134-137
Freud (S.), 95 ff.
Future life, and ethics, 24

God, definition of ethical concepts in terms of, 18, 99-101
Good, meaning of term, 12 ff., 17 ff., 77, Chap. 6 passim, 156-157; kinds of, 66 ff.; as ground of obligation, Chap. 5 passim
Good will, 50 ff.
Guilt, sense of, 97. *v.* Freedom, and Punishment

Hare (R.), 156 n.
Harmony, as the good, 67-68
Hedonism, egoistic, 21-31; psychological, 28-30; universalistic, Chap. 3 passim, 62 n.
Hegel, 55
Hume, 92

Indeterminism, 134-145
Intrinsic goodness, 13 ff., 66 ff., 76-77, 78 ff., 114, 121
Intuition, 27, 115-117, 119-125

Judgements, in ethics, 102 ff., 157
Justice, 45-46, 47, 67; retributive, 145 ff.

Kant, Chap. 4 passim, 125, 129

Love, 51-52, 67
Lying, 38, 53, 56, 58-59, 68 ff., 72

Macdonald (M.), 156 n.
Metaphysics, Ethics, 20, 98 ff.
Mill (J. S.), 37, 42
Moore (G. E.), 32, 42, 61 ff., 63 n., 79 ff., 91, 93
Moral value, 51-52

159

Index

Motives, 25-26, 51 ff., 127, 129 ff.
Naturalism, in Ethics, 82-99, 156
Nowell-Smith (P. H.), 156 n.
Objectivity, of ethics, 102-118
Obligation, 33-34, 77, 92 ff., 100 ff.; prima facie obligations, 72-78
Ought, meanings of term, 15, 63-64, 126, 156; as indefinable, 93

Perry (R. B.), 85
Philosophy, 19-20
Plato, 31, 55, 155
Pleasure, 21-31, Chap. 3 passim, 130; Kant on, 50
Politics, 49, 70, 154-155
Practice, bearing of ethics on, 16-17, 102 ff., 154-155
Prima facie duty, 72 ff.
Primitive peoples, ethics of, 96-97, 112
Progress, in ethics, 125
Promises, 72 ff., 117
Proposition, definition of, 102
Psycho-analysis, 95 ff., 131-132
Psychology, relation to ethics, 82 ff., 95 ff., 98-99, 124-125
Punishment, 97, 139, 145-154

Quality, quantity of pleasure, 42, 47, 50

Reasonableness, 123-125
Religion, 67, 68, 99-101
Ross (Sir David), 72 ff., 129 n., 130 n.

Scepticism, in ethics, 26-27, 98, 110 ff.
Science and ethics, 10-12, 14-15, 81 ff.
Selfishness, Chap. 2 passim
Self-sacrifice, 34-35, 51
Sidgwick (H.), 37
Social Philosophy, 154
Sociological definitions of ethical terms, 88
Socrates, 17
Stealing, 37, 39-40
Stevenson (C. L.), 102 n.
Subconscious, 131-132
Subjective view of Ethics, 102 ff., 156-157

Toulmin (S. E.), 119 n., 156 n.
Truth, of ethical judgements, 102 ff., 118-119, 156-157

Universality, in ethics, 53-59, 125
Unselfishness, Chap. 2 passim
Utilitarianism, hedonistic, Chap. 3 passim, 62 n.; non-hedonistic, 60, Chap. 5 passim

Virtue, 31 ff., 67, 76, 125

War, ethics of, 57 ff., 113-114